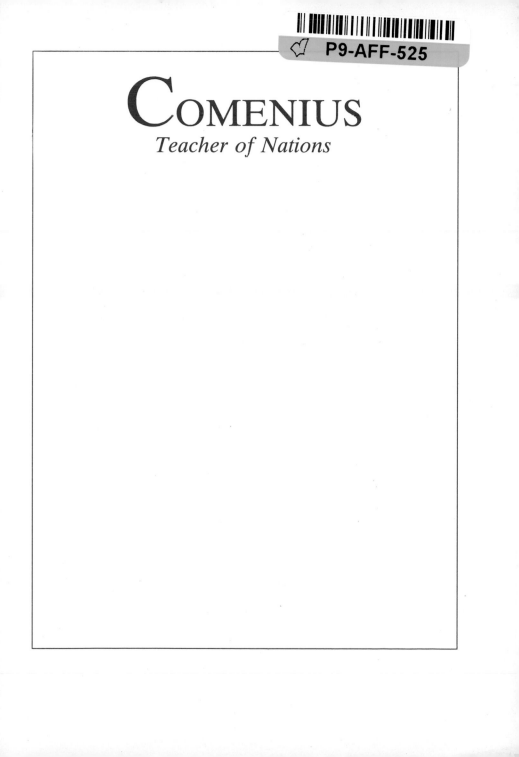

COMENIUS
Teacher of Nations

Jaroslav
PÁNEK

COMENIUS
Teacher of Nations

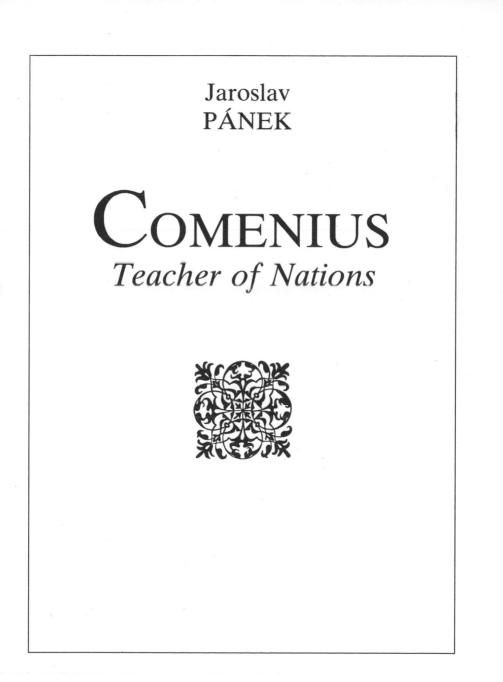

———————————— (JOAN AMOS COMENIUS) ————————————

ISBN   80-234-0045-2
(anglické vydanie)

Table of contents

(JOAN AMOS COMENIUS)

Born Into a Labyrinth

The year 1592 became a symbol of life and death for the Czech nation. Seen from the vantage point of the four centuries that have passed since then, it is radiant with the light of life into which Jan Amos Komenský – better known internationally as Comenius – was born in the extreme southeastern corner of the then Czech state. He was to grow into a man whose unique work brought to the climax all the past cultural development of his nation, the best fruits of which he presented to the world and at the same time gave humanity a hope for a better future, it so badly needed. However, for the people who then lived in that country in the centre of Europe, that year appeared quite different. They sensed great changes in the coming, which were hardly promising for anybody.

The ominous feeling proceeded from more concrete happenings than the dire predictions spreading throughout Europe, that this sinful world would perish with the coming of the new century, in 1600. The Czech people, and especially the residents of the royal seat of Prague, had more serious grounds for real concern. Reports were coming in from the west about the civil war in France, which already since the dreadful St. Bartholomew's Night of 1572 had evoked dreadful anxiety that a similar mass slaughter could also occur in denominationally split Prague. In the east, another major war with the Turks was looming on the horizon, another stage of the continuous battle for Hungary, for which already several generations of Czechs had been forced to pay a heavy toll in money and blood. What was most ominous, however, was that in the Czech State proper, an internal conflict was growing between the ruler and the Estates, the Protestant opposition, between the Catholics and the Protestants, between the ruling minority and the increasingly dissatisfied majority of the population.

These tensions and feelings of insecurity increased precisely in 1592, when magnificent funeral services were held in Prague for the deceased Czech „Viceroy" and the most powerful nobleman in the country, Lord

Vilém of Rožmberk (1535 – 1592). In the very centre of the capital with an overwhelmingly Protestant population, Jesuits – those militant champions of uncompromising and relentless Catholicism – staged a large show of force, fired by hopes to destroy all non-Catholics. Contemporaries well realized that in Rožmberk the country had lost the most prominent representative of traditional religious toleration and political compromise, the likes of whom were so badly needed in the religiously divided country. For all of the second half of the 16th century, tolerant Catholics as well as Protestants viewed their „viceroy" as a champion of justice and felt that there was no other magnate enjoying such natural authority, who could follow in Rožmberk's footsteps. They realized that in this man they had lost „the mainstay of the Czech Kingdom" and that now their country was rushing headlong into destruction.

What was like the country where Comenius was born? What was the source of all the conflicts that had thrown his contemporaries into the darkest pessimism?

Since its founding in the 10th century, the Czech State had undergone a development full of ups and downs, but it preserved its continuity and independent position. In fact, on several occasions its rulers even tried to win a dominant position in Central Europe. Under the rule of the Czech king and Holy Roman Emperor Charles IV (1346 – 1378), the Czech Kingdom did indeed attain this position and consolidated its frontiers which it still had at the time when it was Comenius' home. The hub of the Crown of the Czech Kingdom, which was the official name of the state, was the Czech Kingdom proper with Prague as the capital, and the associated Moravian Mark, Comenius' actual homeland. Their population was overwhelmingly Czech, but gradually a German minority grew in importance, particularly along the kingdom's frontiers. In the north were three more crown lands – the Silesian Princedom and two lesser marks of Upper and Lower Lusatia. There, on the other hand, the population was mostly German, but also included Czechs, Poles and Sorbs. In the course of the 16th century there was an influx into the towns of Italians and other nationals, but the Czech language retained its deep roots in the two principal lands, and its privileged position remained legally safeguarded until the beginning of the 17th century. While occasional conflicts did occur, the ethnic problem was not a serious one in the Czech State. Political and religious differences were of much greater and graver significance.

The line-up of forces in the midst of which young Comenius had found himself was the result of two centuries of earlier development. The historical determinant was the Hussite revolution, itself the product of a profound crisis that had riven mediaeval feudal society and, in particular, the Roman Catholic Church. The crisis was also manifest in other parts of Central and Western Europe, and gave rise to different reform trends, the most outstanding of them reflected in the teachings of the English philosopher John Wyclif (prob. 1320 – 1384) who insisted that the Church should be rid of all property and should return to its apostolic simplicity. Wyclif's ideas found a fertile ground in Bohemia where already in the 14th century the Church had become the biggest landowner, a fact which the nobility and the other strata of society strongly opposed. The Czech reformers' call for a redistribution of material values and for a moral rebirth found an unusually responsive audience and became the ideological foundation of a powerful social movement. It was not stopped even by the condemnation of its most prominent leader, Jan (John) Hus (prob. 1372 – 1415), as heretic by the Council at Konstanz and his subsequent burning at the stake. On the contrary, this act of violence spurred the radicalization of the Hussite movement which embodied the Czech nation's opposition to the Catholic world. In its supreme, revolutionary stage (1419 – 1434), the Hussite movement undermined the power of the Catholic Church fully in Bohemia and partly also in Moravia, and the Church's vast land holdings were seized by the nobility and by the towns. The position of the serfs and the town poor improved only slightly, but the three privileged estates – the higher nobility (the lords), the lesser nobility (the knights), and the free royal towns – immensely strengthened their position. Since this process was parallelled by a decline of the king's authority, the estates – particularly the nobility – acquired the decisive role in legislation, state administration, and the judiciary.

The estates-dominated Czech monarchy obtained from the Hussite revolution not only new economic and political power, but also a lasting ideological heritage. The originally far-reaching ideas of reform were reduced in the course of the revolution and the subsequent decades to a platform acceptable to all adherents of Hussitism, irrespective of their social status. The essence of this platform was the idea that the Church must not dominate the believers and in no respect must elevate itself above them. The Hussites therefore stressed the principle of equality of the clergy and lay persons in communion „in both kinds" – **sub utraque specie** – i.e. both bread and wine as symbols of Christ's body and blood. The drinking of wine from the chalice during communion, earlier reserved only for the clergy, was made accessible to lay Christians, and, making use of this symbol, the Hussites began calling themselves utraquists or „people of the Chalice". However, their original idea that they would attain a universal reform of Christianity, or at least unity of all Czechs on the basis of utraquism, proved to be unrealistic. For various reasons, a minority of the population of Bohemia and Moravia remained loyal to Catholicism, and the Silesians and Lusatians remained practically unaffected by the Hussite movement. Thus, the first – Czech – reformation was only partly successful with the result that in the 15th century the Czech State became a „land of two peoples". Utraquists and Catholics continued to live there side by side, but the latter mostly enjoyed the support of the kings and their fellow-believers abroad. The utraquist Czechs did repel all foreign interventions and retained their numerical superiority in the two key lands of the Czech State, but for most of a century they became a symbol of heresy in Central Europe.

This split into two denominations was not the final outcome of the Czech reformation. Many Hussites did not accept the compromise and frequently inconsistent ideology of the utraquists, and associated themselves in a special community – the Unity, or Community of Brethren. When established in 1457, it was a church of the poor and the oppressed. Its members pledged themselves to voluntary poverty, rejected force and violence, and were resolved not to resist evil. A very pronounced feature of the Brethren was firm discipline which was maintained in the Community's congregations until the 17th century. By placing such strict demands on its members, as well as by its lofty ideals, the Community unwittingly chose to remain a highly selective religious community rather than to grow – even in the Czech environment – into a major church. Nevertheless, gradually the Community of Brethren won the favour of part of the burghers and the nobility. In the course of time, even some Czech and Moravian lords became its adherents and thereby gave it at first unrealized authority within society. After 1480, when the Brethren abandoned the rule of voluntary poverty, the Community was also open to wealthy and influential people. However, even the subsequent influx into its ranks of burghers and the nobility failed to secure legitimacy for the Community. The Community of Brethren was not included in the religious peace concluded between the Catholics and the utraquists in 1485, and was repeatedly banned by occasional royal decrees. The Brethren, especially those from the non-privileged classes, were being persecuted, some were exiled, and their houses of prayer were being closed by force. Nevertheless, the weakness of royal power and the growth of de facto religious tolerance in post-Hussite Bohemia prevented the total uprooting of the Community. However, its members grew accustomed over several generations to legal and existential security, and thus were much better prepared during Comenius' time for patient and disciplined resistance than the numerically much more powerful Utraquists.

The 16th century brought profound changes to Comenius' native land. Additional waves of the reformation swept Europe – first the Lutheran and then the Calvinist. Both these reform trends met with great response in the Czech Kingdom because most of the ethnic German population now embraced Luther's teachings, while the Czechs viewed these teachings as a confirmation and concrete realization of the Hussite principles. Most Czech Utraquists found new encouragement for more radical policies and strove for the establishment of a Czech church of the Lutheran type. The Community of Brethren, too, found interest in the new tenets and sent its students to Lutheran universities while carefully guarding and maintaining its identity. It was only in the second half of the 16th century, when it began to establish closer contacts with the Swiss reformation and found its fellow--believers abroad among the reformed Calvinists. Thus, when Comenius was born, his country offered a most varied and mostly also confusing confessional and political picture. The population of Bohemia proper consisted of some 80 % Utraquists and Lutherans, about 10 % Catholics, 5 – 10 % adherents of the outlawed Community of Brethren, and some Calvinists and members of lesser religious sects. In Moravia, which enjoyed greater religious tolerance, this denominational mosaic was still more colourful because in addition to all the aforesaid churches, it offered haven to a large-scale influx of persecuted Anabaptists, as well as to Anti-Trinitarians and members of many other religious groups. In Silesia and Lusatia, Lutherans gained the majority.

While papal diplomats referred to Moravia as to a chaotic breeding ground of countless heresies, its inhabitants lived next to each other in rather good concord. The same was true of the other lands of the Czech Kingdom. The common people grew increasingly tolerant towards each other, while many of their feudal masters became magnanimously indifferent to the religious beliefs and denomination of their subjects, recognizing their right to a free choice of confession. However, from the viewpoint of state power, this advanced religious differentiation was one of the main obstacles to strengthening the ruler's authority. This fact gained prominence after Ferdinand I of the House of Hapsburg ascended to the Czech throne in 1526, and began realizing his plan of uniting the Czech, Austrian, and Hungarian states into a centralized monarchy.

This official Hapsburg policy ran right from the beginning into opposition of the estates, fearing a curtailment of their political rights, and into resistance of the non-Catholics against a purposeful re-Catholization drive. The Hapsburg doctrine was based on the idea that a coherent monarchy could be built only if its population were religiously united, and thus all available means were being used to suppress the other, non-Catholic churches. Therefore, the very first anti-Hapsburg uprising in Bohemia in 1547 combined defence of the estates' rights with defence of religious freedom, and thus, quite naturally, noblemen from the Community of Brethren stood at the head of the radical insurgents. The Community's members were thrown into prison, their property was being confiscated and they themselves forced into exile, and all of the Community's houses of prayer were closed. The Brethren left for Moravia and also established a large centre of the Community's exiles abroad, in the Polish town of Leszno where Comenius, too, found haven many years later. The nobility from the Community of Brethren remained also in the future one of the mainstays of the anti-Hapsburg resistance, and was treated accordingly by the Hapsburg rulers.

It was beyond the power of the Hapsburg sitting on the Czech throne to carry out a forcible re-Catholization of the Czech State. But behind the Central European branch of the Hapsburg family stood the power and wealth of the Spanish line of the Hapsburgs who had gained hegemony over Western Europe and who had extended their „world empire" to their colonies in America. The Central European Hapsburg also had the backing of the papacy and of the entire Catholic Church which after the Council of Trident (1545 – 1563) had set out on a road of internal reconstruction and recapture of its lost positions. On more than one occasion, papal diplomats had stressed that the decisive factor for the future of Catholicism was a reversal of the situation in Bohemia, and for the Hapsburgs, too, this country – the most important of their possessions in Central Europe – was a key to success. Thus, the offensive of Catholicism in Europe focussed on the Czech Kingdom where much greater tension was building up than in the neighbouring countries.

Formally, the Hapsburgs insisted on preserving the legally established system of two confessions – Catholicism and Utraquism (but in its archaic form, long abandoned by neo-Utraquists) – and refused to accept any change. This instituted legality reflected the long outdated situation in the 15th century and stood in sharp contradiction to the confessional and political reality of the second half of the 16th century. The non-Catholic estates in Bohemia long sought a way out of the untenable situation and eventually found it in unity of the majority of Utraquists with members of the Community of Brethren on the basis of the Czech Confession. This confession, drawn up in 1575, was formulated so broadly as to cover the neo-Utraquists, Lutherans and the Czech Brethren who, moreover, could retain their own confession and rules. At the time when religious conflicts were reaching their climax in Europe, this was a remarkable example of ecumenism. The Czech Confession was not recognized by the ruler, but it succeeded in rallying ideologically and organizationally the broad non--Catholic opposition to the point where it established a platform for a continued struggle for its very existence.

In the last quarter of the 16th century, it was still possible to uphold for some time the fragile balance between the ruler and his Catholic adherents on one side, and the non-Catholic opposition of the other side. Much depended on how far the highest officials of the kingdom could maintain peace and order and prevent provoking the non-Catholics by insensitive administrative moves. But it was precisely in 1592, when the death of the most influential of the Czech lords, Vilém of Rožmberk, almost symbolically ended the role played in Czech history by the last conciliatory generation of the high Catholic nobility, which placed common interests of the Czech lands and of the estates above confessional differences. The new generation of Catholic politicians, raised by Jesuits in the spirit of uncompromising re-Catholization, was prepared to provoke a conflict with the non-Catholics in the firm belief that it would prevail for its own benefit. At the end of the 16th century these radicals entered the Czech government and assumed all executive power. Their first measures included renewed persecution of the Community of Brethren. The non-Catholics now lost their support not only in the ruler and the government, but also in a manipulated diet and in the courts. The two centuries old dualist division of power was denied and a major conflict was inevitable.

The conflict was averted for some time by a crisis within the Hapsburg dynasty, which stopped the re-Catholization drive for six years between

1606 and 1612. A struggle for the throne between the mentally imbalanced emperor Rudolf II and his younger brother Matthias enabled the estates in the Czech lands to re-assert some of their lost power. In 1609, the Czech estates forced the enactment of religious freedom for adherents of the Czech Confession (including the Community of Brethren), obtained supervision over the administration of the non-Catholic church organization and over Prague University, the main centre of Utraquist ideology. This was a tremendous victory for religious tolerance because freedom of confession was also granted to the commoners, but the equality of the minority Catholics was in no way denied. Nevertheless, the Catholics retained their decisive position in the government and from the very beginning consciously violated the new religious law. The Czech estates were fully aware of this weak point and therefore began – regardless of the de facto hostile government – to build up their own executive power in the form of an assembly of thirty directors, instituted an independent assembly of the estates, convened by non-Catholic „defensors", and strove for the creation of an independent army and finances. Under the onslaught of the radical Catholics associated around the Hapsburg court, and under the impact of the desperate defence of the non-Catholics the country's political system in fact disintegrated. A Protestant „state within a state" came into being and the dissatisfied majority was ready to respond to the provocations of the ruling minority by force and armed resistance. It was only a matter of time when the decisive clash and the solution of the problem of governmental power in Bohemia would take place.

The estates in the other lands of the Czech Crown were not exposed to such a strong re-Catholization drive, but their position as well was deteriorating since the end of the 16th century. While the Silesians established a close alliance with the Czechs and together with them secured legitimacy of religious freedom for Lutherans, the Moravians chose a different line of policy. They joined the anti-Hapsburg opposition in Hungary and in Austria, and with its support brought about a change in the power situation in their province. They placed at the head of the government as provincial governor Karel the Elder of Žerotín (1564 – 1636) a prominent magnate and member of the Community of Brethren, who at that very time became the patron of Comenius. The Moravians firmly insisted on the principle of unrestricted religious freedom, proceedings from the tenet that faith was a gift of God and therefore should not be regulated by law. They relied on the fact that a leader of the non-Catholics as the head of government could better secure the realization of their aspirations than a royal charter. In contrast to the Czech model of formally enacted freedom, they placed their stakes on true freedom protected by executive power of the estates. However, they did not prevent a clash with the ruler in this way either. After 1612, the Hapsburgs consolidated their position and power in their monarchy and resumed their earlier re-Catholization drive. In 1615 they forced Žerotín the Elder to resign and to retire to the privacy of his family holdings, while with the help of the Catholic radicals in Bohemia, they escalated their conflict with the Czech estates to the razor's edge. Their provocations caused an uprising and war in the period 1618 – 1620, which engulfed the entire Czech State.

Naturally, the young years of Comenius were not filled only with struggle for religious freedom, the split and eventual destruction of the system of estates, and the threat of war, although it was these very phenomena, which added the character of a special drama to the conflicts of those days. The disintegration of the existing social relationships and forms of government was parallelled by changes in all other spheres of human life. The transition from the relatively peaceful 16th century to the war-ridden 17th century was marked by a feverish formation of mutually hostile alliances; on the one side was the tight Hapsburg-Catholic alliance, and on the other side the looser association of states of an anti-Hapsburg orientation, which included a number of Protestant states but also Catholic France. The European system of states was obviously acquiring a new shape, and it also became apparent that local wars could explode into an all-European conflict with disastrous consequences.

Everybody was affected by economic shocks. They hit the Western, more advanced countries proceeding towards capitalism, just as the countries of Central and Eastern Europe, where the prevailing trend was to strengthen the feudal system of production and organization of society. The turn of the century saw the end of an extended agrarian boom which was replaced by a period of economic depression and disintegration of the existing monetary systems. A universal feeling of insecurity and expectation of further economic blows were reflected in the gradual replacement of the harmonious Renaissance by manneristic culture. Intellectuals lost their faith in the authorities of the Antiquity and their hope for the development of a free human being, and came to realize the horrors of insecurity and weakness of the individual in the turbulent current of history. Man found himself in an earlier unknown maze of socio-political relationships, in a situation appearing incomprehensible to human reason and uncontrollable by human force. At this crossroads of traditional faith and critical reason, many of those swept by the tide of events found themselves at the point of resignation and came to believe that the administration of public affairs had to be left to God.

The idea of a hopelessly incomprehensible human „labyrinth" was not a novel one, but it became the key term for expressing the existing reality only for the generation that lived at the end of the 16th century. It was this „labyrinth of the world" which was also entered by the boy named Jan who was born to miller Martin Segeš Komenský and his wife Anna in the lovely region of Southeastern Moravia, in the town of Uherský Brod, or its close vicinity, on March 28, 1592. A stubborn, persistent and painful search of the way out of this labyrinth became his fate.

The Star of Czech Culture

In 1592 and 1593, Moravia was visited by the noted English traveller Fynes Moryson. In his notes he heaped praise on this charming and fertile land and on its kind and hospitable people. He was fortunate to have seen Moravia at the very end of a period of economic progress and peace, which also benefited the Komenský family. Comenius' father Martin was a prosperous inhabitant of the town of Uherský Brod where he owned a house, a farm and fields. He lived under the benevolent rule of the Lords of Kunovice, who offered protection to the Community of Brethren and stood above confessional disputes, pursuing in their dominion a magnanimous policy of religious coexistence. There was every indication that little Jan, the Komenský's only son, would lead a peaceful and rather prosperous life.

However, the end of the 16th and the beginning of the 17th century brought anxiety even to the Moravian countryside. Just as Bohemia, Moravia, too, became the stage for the struggle between the Catholic government and the Protestant opposition, and was drawn into the large conflict that swept all of Central Europe. Comenius' birthplace lay close to the frontier of the Hungarian Kingdom where an anti-Hapsburg uprising erupted in 1604. The Hungarian insurgents were led by Stefan Bocskai, a Transylvanian magnate who wanted to attract to his side also the estates in the adjoining countries. His slogans of battle for a free homeland and for religious freedom were certainly attractive, but the methods he used in that battle were repulsive. Bocskai tried to carry the civil war in Hungary over into Moravia and sent there his troops which mercilessly plundered the country. The Moravian estates, irrespective of their religious denomination, resisted the invasion but were unable to prevent heavy losses suffered mainly by their subjects. Comenius, who had lost his parents already in 1604 and was left to the care of his relatives, most painfully witnessed these horrors. In May 1605, he saw his temporary home, the small town of Strážnice go up in flames, and almost immediately thereafter the Hungarian troops plundered his patrimony, the farmstead at Uherský Brod. At the age of thirteen, the most sensitive period of adolescence, Comenius experienced at first hand the horrors of war, and his material security was suddenly shaken as well.

It was perhaps the material losses which led to the decision that young Comenius would not follow in his father's footsteps. Doubtlessly, he did not mind, for already at the school in Strážnice he felt the desire for more learning, but also the restlessness and indecisiveness of youth. „I knew not what to do," he wrote later about those days at school. The school run by the Community of Brethren in the small town could hardly endow him with more than trivial knowledge of writing, reading and arithmetic, together with the fundamentals of religion and music. However, a moral counterweight of this intellectual mediocrity were the great demands placed on the cohesion of the Community. The Community's tradition led not only the clergymen but all members towards mutual responsibility, self-improvement, and participation in „universal priesthood". This was a great inspiration for a perceptive student. Evolving it with the help of subsequently acquired knowledge no longer had anything in common with small-town practicism, but injected a new meaning into education as an instrument for the future reform of human society.

Even the Community's school in Přerov, though one of the best in Moravia, could fully satisfy Comenius' thirst for knowledge. There, too, conservatism survived, coupled with mediocrity and persistent efforts to preserve the Community's exclusiveness, which frequently resulted in rejection of higher education and new ideas. Nevertheless the period he spent at Přerov between 1608 and 1611, meant very much for the young man. If nothing else, it gave him the belated opportunity to learn Latin and to establish an intellectual contact with the world. It also enabled him to establish closer contacts with the Community's spiritual and secular leaders. Among them, especially Bishop Jan Lanecius and the prominent Moravian magnate Karel the Elder of Žerotín detected Comenius' exceptional talent and became the young man's patrons.

Of course, even the quiet backwaters of the Přerov school were stirred by echoes of bitter confessional strife and theological polemics. Its students secretly obtained a Latin catechism which helped them understand Socinian teachings. Their denial of Christ's divinity, the mainstay of Christian dogma, attracted Comenius and his fellow-students as sensational reading, but he himself was profoundly shocked. Although the teacher of Latin soon discovered and burned the „heretical" book, he could no longer save his most perceptive student from a deep internal crisis which – as Comenius himself later said – it took him several years to overcome. However, the decision had already been made on Comenius' future profession. His patrons saw his school training as preparation for his eventual priesthood. Therefore, they sent the nineteen-year old young man, who had been given the Biblical name Amos at Přerov, to study in Germany.

Since the turn of the century, the Community's foremost intellectuals strongly tended towards the teachings of Swiss reformers, Calvinism in particular. Therefore, in Comenius' case, too, they chose not the much closer Lutheran universities, but the distant „Nassau Academy" at Herborn. There, Comenius found himself in quite a different intellectual environment than his native Moravia could offer him. A prominent member of the Herborn faculty was Johann Heinrich Alsted, one of the best known philosophers and theologians of the early 17th century. It was he, too, who wielded the strongest influence on Comenius. He impressed the young man by his bold endeavour to compile the findings of all sciences into a large encyclopaedic work, as well as by his effort to classify all knowledge and to place human findings into harmony with Biblical revelations. Although Alsted was not an original thinker, he was interested in natural sciences as well as in the „secret sciences" (alchemy, astrology, the cabala, etc.), and transmitted this Renaissance inquisitiveness to his pupil. On the other hand, Johannes Fischer-Piscator sparked in Comenius the effort to master thoroughly the Bible, just as the belief in the coming of Christ's millenial realm (chiliasm) which was to produce a universal reform of all things human. Of no lesser significance for understanding the contemporary social and political situation were the views of the fomer Herborn professor Johann Heinrich Althusius on the state and government. It was Althusius who claimed that a just state must be based on corporations of the estates and that in such state contractually entrusted power must be divided between the ruler and the estates. In this respect his views were close to the recent political practice in Moravia, which, however, was already being crushed by the Hapsburg centralization drive, and indirectly supported the ideas held by the radical leaders of the estates in the Czech lands.

Thus, the two years he spent at Herborn (1611 – 1613) helped Comenius to make up for the time he had lost and to absorb the heritage of European humanism. They also encouraged his own literary activity even though it took the form of so far minor writings containing no original ideas of his own. What was most important, of course, was that his stay and study at Herborn gave him much spiritual inspiration to which he returned throughout his life and from which proceeded in his own, original way.

From Herborn, considered something of an advance post of the revolutionary Netherlands on German soil, Comenius went in 1613 to the United Dutch Provinces. There he visited for the first time Amsterdam, the city which was to become his last haven at the end of his life. Just as other Czech and Moravian travellers of those days, he saw the Netherlands at the peak of that country's economic and cultural development. He saw the advantages of the Dutch-Protestant civilization, which he embraced for the rest of his life. However, he soon returned to Germany to continue his studies at Heidelberg University. A letter of recommendation from professor Piscator opened the door for him to the Heidelberg theologian David Pareus who attracted Comenius' interest with his efforts to reconcile the differences existing between Protestant churches. Besides the tradition of peaceful coexistence of different confessions in his native Moravia, this was another important inspiration for Comenius' later ecumenical endeavours.

In the spring of 1614, Comenius returned home full of impressions and resolutions. On his long journey back, made on foot, he visited for the first and last time Prague which was already losing its former glory of imperial residence of Rudolf II, and of a centre of mannerist science and the arts. On the other hand, he found in the Czech capital his co-religionists from the Community of Brethren in a new position. Since the issue of a Decree on Religious Freedom (1609), they formed a fully legitimate church in Bohemia and preached their sermons in the famous Bethlehem Chapel where John Hus used to preach. The Community was now acting publicly as the carrier of the Hussite heritage and bore co-responsibility for the general cultural standard. It had to cope with the effects of its long years of isolation and wanted to catch up as quickly as possible with the more advanced countries of Europe. In Comenius it acquired a personality who wanted to devote his youthful energy and enthusiasm to the spiritual emancipation of his nation.

In the light of the encyclopaedic and irenical efforts of his German teachers, young Comenius saw the world as a perfect divine creation. He was convinced that „the supremely good Lord does all things extremely well and artfully", but this lofty belief sharply contrasted with the situation

in his country which had once stood in the forefront of European knowledge and culture, but in which Comenius now missed works comparable
to what he had seen in Germany and the Netherlands. „I was seized by true
love of my dear homeland and by sorrow and pain over the lassitude
of my fellow-countrymen," he complained shortly after his return to Moravia. He saw many tasks waiting for him and set out to deal with them
with remarkable consistency and dedication.

The first place where he could assert himself in practice was the school
in Přerov where he returned as a teacher now. Remembering his negative
experiences as a student, he began to strive – to use his own words – „for
a more pleasant method of educating children". He compared the traditional Community system of education mainly with the ideas of the German
educator Wolfgang Ratke (Ratichius), finding similarities – especially
in the accent placed on the irreplaceable role of the mother tongue – but
also differences which favoured the Ratichian educational reform. It was
in this sense that he wanted to facilitate instruction of foreign languages,
Latin in particular, and strove for an informal and descriptive education
of all youth. However, he also began to realize quite clearly the link
between a pupil's theoretical preparation and his practical tasks as well
as with public activity, and sought the desirable harmony between the
school, the church community, and the political instruments for guiding
interhuman relations.

The first results were soon to appear in the form of the textbook „Rules
of Easier Grammar Instruction" (**Grammaticae facilioris praecepta**), printed in Prague in 1616. Unfortunately, no copy of the book has been
preserved. Mastering the grammar was not the end objective of instruction
for Comenius, but only one of essential instruments. However, from the
very beginning, language as a means of communication played in his ideas
an important role as the key to the basic problems of theory and practice,
and as an instrument of true understanding between individuals and nations. Comenius wanted nothing less than defining the structure of the
language which he viewed as a reflection of the ideology of every nation.
Already in the course of his studies he began work on a large dictionary
of his mother tongue, the Treasury of the Czech Language (**Thesaurus
linguae Bohemicae**). He wanted to show in it the lexical and stylistic
potential of the Czech language so that in the future it would be possible
to translate any highly polished Latin text into its Czech equivalent and
vice versa without any detriment to the message of its content. The accent

placed on the communicative and socio-organizational role of the language thus extended beyond the framework of the national culture and served as inspiration for thoughts about unification of humanity on the basis of universal education.

Comenius viewed as another prerequisite for overcoming the bounds of provincionalism the necessity of raising the level of real knowledge. This meant classification and blending of all the attained knowledge from natural science to history and philosophy. He wanted to present to the Czech public an impressively conceived encyclopaedia of two main divisions. The first one – The Theatre of the Universe (**Theatrum universitatis rerum**) – was to have covered the universe and nature, the world's geography, and an outline of human history. The second division – The Theatre of the Script (**Theatrum divinum**) – was to cover the sacral world and Biblical history, as well as matters of ethics and postmortal salvation. Realizing such a project would have naturally called for a tremendous effort and much preparatory work.

After having outlined his concept, Comenius also proceeded to deal with partial tasks whereby he came into close contact with the social problems of his native land. He realized that so far nobody had produces a solid outline of Moravian history and took up historiographical research. He found support with his patron, Karel the Elder of Žerotín, who was an advocate of a specifically provincial patriotism and was seeking arguments for his political strategy in the past of his land as well. There is every indication that he opened to the young teacher the rich family archives and library, who repaid his kindness with his Moravian Antiquities and with the treatise The History and the Deeds of the Lords of Žerotín. These works, which have not been preserved, were probably not outstanding pieces of scholarly criticism, but strengthened the self-esteeem of the Moravian estates and parallelled the more advanced Czech provincial historiography where, by the way, it was also the Community of Brethren that had seized the initiative somewhat earlier. By his research work, Comenius laid the foundations for Moravian historiography and geography, and made a successful attempt to depict his native land in a map published in Amsterdam in 1627 and providing the most reliable cartographic data about Moravia until the beginning of the 18th century.

Comenius' manifold programme of scholarly humanism was not being realized as rapidly as he would have wished. Personal and public affairs and events forced him to take a position on the growing social and political conflicts as well. After he had been ordained in 1616 and two years later appointed pastor of the Community's congregation and headmaster of its school in the North Moravian town of Fulnek, Comenius had to settle differences and mutual complaints between the well-to-do and the poor members of the congregation. He reacted to them in his sermones and in the treatise Letters to Heavens, written in 1619. He knew too well the dire situation of the urban poor than to deny unjust distribution of wealth. But he was too far removed from the original social ideas of his church which in the 15th century required from its members voluntary poverty. Nor did he reach so far the belief in the desirability of social equality among Christians. Although he showed a profound sympathy with the suffering and sharply criticized the selfishness of the rich, he was still unable to abandon his ideas of prevailing harmony. He could only plead in the words of Christ for love among Christians, for charity on the part of the rich and powerful, as well as for patience on the part of the poor and the oppressed.

At the threshold of the Thirty Years' War, social contradictions were overshadowed by the looming conflict between the Hapsburg-Catholic and the anti-Hapsburg and Protestant worlds which also split the Czech and Moravian society into two irreconcilable camps. Comenius, most probably with some co-authors, responded to this religious and political tension with a treatise entitled Protection Against Anti-Christ and His Trials, and published in 1617. At the time when there was only minuscule hope left for understanding, Comenius departed from the tactics of compromise, so persistently pursued by Karel the Elder of Žerotín, and called for a struggle against the Papacy and the Jesuits. This struggle was to be waged not only on the European scale but also within a regional framework. In Moravia it was to attain secularization of church property, which would have meant undermining the power of the Bishop of Olomouc, the largest land owner in the country and at the same time the most relentless opponent of the Community of Brethren. The Protection suggested that the grandiose programme of Czech and Moravian scholarly humanism would have to give way for some time to political struggle which Comenius the priest and teacher also wanted to enter.

The Czech uprising which between 1618 and 1620 climaxed the estates' resistance against the Hapsburgs did not meet with unequivocal response in Moravia. The most influential magnate and Community leader Karel the Elder of Žerotín saw the uprising as lost in advance, and therefore remained loyal to the Hapsburg dynasty. For many of his coreligionists he became a traitor, and even Comenius did not share his views. Influenced by Althusius, he sympathized with the creation in 1619 of a new state formation, the Czech Confederation, since it succeeded in linking on a voluntary basis all the five lands of the Czech Crown through constitutional equality of their status in overcoming the centuries-old rivalry between the estates of the individual lands. The full religious freedom of the Protestants did not remove tolerance towards the Catholic minority, and in the cultural sphere, too, earlier inconceivable opportunities emerged. No wonder then, that Comenius sided with the confederated estates and that he took part in welcoming the newly elected king, Friedrich of the Palatinate. He knew already during his studies at Heidelberg, that Friedrich stood at the head of the anti-Hapsburg forces in the Holy Roman Empire, and as many of his contemporaries hoped for substantial help from Friedrich's father-in-law, the English king James I Stuart.

However, these hopes were brutally shattered. James I turned away from the rebels, the solidarity shown by the Netherlands was insufficient, and the confederated countries soon exhausted by the war against the Hapsburgs. Their two drives against imperial Vienna failed, while the invasion of Bohemia by the Hapsburgs and their allies attained its objective. The disastrous defeat of the Czech estates on White Mountain near Prague on November 8, 1620, demonstrated the military superiority of the enemy and at the same time disclosed the insufficient social base of the resistance movement. The uprising in Bohemia quickly collapsed, while in Moravia and Silesia attempts continued for some time yet to stem the Hapsburg onslaught. This continued fighting moved the stage of the horrors of war to Moravia. In the spring of 1621, the imperial troops also entered Fulnek and burned it down.

The horrors of war were parallelled by restoration of Hapsburg power which behaved in Bohemia and Moravia as in conquered lands deprived of all their rights and privileges. The Holy Roman Emperor and King of Bohemia Ferdinand II abolished all the achievements of the past years and launched a policy of forcible re-Catholization with the intention of making the entire population profess the only permitted faith and instituting confessional absolutism. The first victims of persecution included priests of the Community of Brethren who in October 1621 were expelled from Moravia. Among them was also Comenius who for a long time refused to accept this fate. He hoped that the remnants of the internal opposition or a military intervention from abroad by the anti-Hapsburg forces would restore religious freedom in his native country. He preferred living in hiding where he tried to continue his literary work. Karel the Elder of Žerotín understood his adherence to the rebels and because he himself was not being persecuted due to his loyalty to the Hapsburgs, he provided to Comenius shelter on his estate at Brandýs nad Orlicí in Eastern Bohemia. However, not even there was Comenius spared the suffering he felt when hearing negative reports from the battlefields. Moreover, he suffered a personal tragedy when his wife Magdalena and his two little sons, who had stayed in Fulnek, all died of the plague. Thus, the year 1622 marked the end once and forever of the happier period of Comenius' life. Soon thereafter, in May 1623, his library was publicly burned on the Fulnek town square; Bonaventura, a fanatical Capuchin monk, made schoolchildren watch the dismal event. Moravia, now dominated by Catholic radicals, thereby denounced the humanistic programme of its great son.

Nevertheless, Comenius would not give up. He drew still closer to the leadership of his endangered church which offered him comfort as well as a new family. In September 1624, he married Marie Dorota, the daughter of the Community's bishop Jan Cyrill. Cyrill was the man who only five years earlier placed the Czech royal crown on the head of Friedrich of the Palatinate and who retained close contacts with the leading political exiles. Comenius joined him in considering ways of saving the Community and with his help undertook several long journeys. His task was to win support for the Community's members abroad and, if necessary, to prepare a new centre of the Community's activities not far from the Czech frontier. Thus, in 1625 and 1626 Comenius travelled to Poland and Brandenburg, and even as far as the Netherlands to meet King Friedrich. In addition, he took the risk of returning to Moravia in order to arrange the transfer of the Community's printing shop and of the library of Karel the Elder of Žerotín to a safe place. In the meantime the Hapsburgs had consolidated their power in Bohemia and Moravia to the point where even the Community's protectors in the ranks of the nobility could remain in their country. Comenius had to leave abroad with his family and with the Cyrill family and the Sádovskýs of Sloupno who had sheltered him in their manor at Bílá Třemešná between 1626 and 1628. It was February 1628, and Comenius' new home was to be Leszno in Poland.

Comenius spent the years that had passed between the disaster on White

Mountain and his departure into exile by intensive literary work. However, he was unable to pursue his earlier work focussed on gathering and classification of knowledge about a harmonious world. Nor could he write brief critical essays and appeals because in the midst of war they appeared insignificant and senseless. The accumulating tragic news and reports, which parallelled his own, personal tragedy and the disaster that befell his nation so depressed Comenius, that he felt all his earlier securities fall apart. He was able only for some time to comfort himself and those closest to him with „writings of consolation" in which he humbly placed himself into the hands of the Almighty.

During the several years he spent in hiding, Comenius vacillated between tense expectations when the anti-Hapsburg coalition was gaining strength, and deep pessimism when the rising hope was shattered over and over again; he wavered between creative activity and doubts about the sense of any human work. He depicted his inner drama with unusual artistic force in the first two volumes of his work Despondent (1622 – 1624), in which, as the principal character, he converse with Reason and Faith. He recalled painfully how „brutal and bloodstained sword destroys my beloved country, . . . my poor people are being oppressed, tortured, . . . murdered and imprisoned, . . . God's truth is being suppressed, pure divine services are being prohibited, priests driven out or thrown in gaol". Seeing the endless and senseless destruction of material and spiritual values, he found no consolation in any rational or religious grounds. The reality he experienced placed in doubt even his deeply rooted faith. The only relief was offered by the words of Christ about the proximity of his second coming. After such mainstays of Comenius' cultural programme, as encyclopaedism, irenism and others had been shaken, the only thing left was the living and steadily growing chiliastic faith in the coming of the kingdom of God. This belief helped Comenius overcome his temporary scepticism and encouraged him in his endeavour to help bring about such universal reform.

In the newly emerged perspective, the scholastic concept of the world as foreordained and efficiently arranged, as Comenius had specified it in his Theatre, was being swept away. After so many shocks which cast in doubt all that had been learned so far, there was no way out but to re-assess the entire reality of life. Comenius well realized that more was involved than the tragedy of the Czech nation alone. Already the beginning of the Thirty Years' War convinced him that all of Europe had sunk into a deep crisis. Therefore, as an allegorical Pilgrim, he set out on a tour of the world, symbolized by an urban labyrinth, and since he had the gift of seeing otherwise than through the customary glasses of confusion, he discovered everywhere fraud, lies, hypocrisy, and evil. There was no perfection to be seen anywhere and, on the contrary, everything was confused and deprived of all sense. However, Comenius' objective was more than superficial verbal criticism. He wanted to make an emotional assessment of all components of human society and of all its organizational forms which individually and in their sum total did not meet the needs of humanity. The Labyrinth of the World and the Paradise of the Heart, written in 1623, tied by its social criticism onto the tradition of European Utopias, in particular the work of the German humanist Johann Valentin Andreae. However, it did not present a new Utopian vision which would try once and forever to solve all social problems. While Comenius, too, did not avoid an indication of the ideal („paradise of the heart"), conceived in the spirit of the Community's traditions, but he strove mainly for a radical departure from a rigid concept of the world and suggested the necessity of seeking new ways for improving human society.

The Labyrinth was the climax of Comenius' literary work and of that part of his work written in his mother tongue. It was the most profound and also artistically most mature work of older Czech literature, which under extreme circumstances blended together the contemporary currents of Czech and European humanism. At the same time it reflected besides Comenius' outstanding literary talent also his thoughts on preaching, poesy, and theory of Czech literature in general. Although his original idea about culminating the programme of Czech humanism was quite different, it was precisely by this work that he put the stamp of worldliness on Czech humanism. At the same time he indicated the potential of Czech culture and its development, had it not been forcibly interrupted by the consequences of the defeat on White Mountain and the exile of the foremost personalities of Czech learning and culture.

The author of the Labyrinth appeared on the skies of Czech culture like a brilliant star shortly before they fell into darkness for two centuries. He wanted to rid Czech culture of mediocrity and provincialism, but after he had left into exile, it sank deeply below the standard it had in the 16th century. Nevertheless, Comenius took his high standard along. The tragedy he had experienced was the price he paid for his inner transformation from a passive observer and describer of the world to an active champion

of humanity's reform. As the contemporary Czech philosopher and Come-
niologist Pavel Floss has most aptly demonstrated, the Labyrinth already
encoded the turn from the theatre of things to the drama of man.

The Exile

Following the institution of confessional absolutism, as it was embodied in the Reconstructed Provincial Constitution for Bohemia and Moravia from 1627 and 1628, there was no place left for the Czech Brethren and other non-Catholics in their own country. Large numbers of noblemen, burghers and priests emigrated to the neighboring Protestant countries, but the serfs, who had no right to leave, had to flee secretly from their Catholic masters. Droves of exiles moved to the east, to Hungary, and to the north, to Poland, Saxony and Brandenburg, but also went further west, to the Netherlands. Most of the exiles hoped that their forced departure was not permanent and that the situation would change, permitting them to return home sooner or later.

Comenius, too, shared this hope and did not want to move far away, so that he could quickly return and work on the reconstruction of his ravished country. His choice was the main centre of the Brethren's émigrés, the town of Leszno which lay on Polish territory very close to the Czech frontier. He had been to Leszno already in the summer of 1625 in order to investigate the local situation. At that time, the town did indeed offer the best possible conditions for the émigrés. It was one of the thriving economic and cultural centres of southwestern Poland, and its population of more than 10,000 made it a relatively large urban community in that part of Europe. The Leszczyński family, who were the lords of Leszno, were known for their religious tolerance and after the defeat of the anti-Hapsburg rebellion of 1547 accommodated the first wave of exiled Brethren in the conviction that the Community was the purest Christian church. In fact, they themselves joined it, but also protected other non-Catholics – especially Calvinists, Lutherans, and Socinians – and provided them with good conditions for their new life. Well-advanced handicraft production and long-distance trade created a favourable material background for the cultural life of the Polish, Czech and German population. A special place was held in this sphere by Leszno's **gymnasium illustre** which was to become Comenius' new place of work.

Comenius' and his family were accompanied on their way to exile by a seventeen-year old girl who symbolized the link between the Community's Czech and Polish members and who profoundly influenced Comenius' future thinking. She was Kristina, the daughter of Julian Poniatowski, a Community priest of Polish origin; This girl of poor health had attracted attention already prior to her departure from Bohemia, and later in Poland, by her frequent seizures when she lost consciousness and spoke – as some people believed – with God's voice. She foretold an early fall of the Catholic enemies – the Pope, the Hapsburgs and their supreme military commander, the Czech nobleman Albrecht of Wallenstein. Some of her predictions did materialize, for example about the fall of the Duke of Wallenstein, who was murdered in 1634 on orders of Emperor Ferdinand II. However, most of Kristina's predictions were merely reflections of the wishful thinking of the girl's Protestant exiles, and some of them were highly critical of the visions. Comenius, on the contrary, firmly believed that his charge was indeed, transmitting secret, divine messages when unconscious. He tried to promote his belief in prophecies by publishing Kristina's and other revelations in Czech and Latin books; he did not even hesitate to transmit some prophecies (of the Silesian tanner Christoph Kotter) to ex-king Friedrich of the Palatinate already in 1626 in order to encourage him to engage in more effective anti-Hapsburg activities.

Comenius was criticized for this folly for more than three hundred years, and the revelations were even viewed as a dark spot in his work. Only most recent research has considered this question from a different angle. Undoubtedly, by his approach to prophecies, Comenius tied onto the ancient traditions of pre-critical thinking, and his interpretations failed to convince many of his contemporaries. He himself underwent a profound change of views on revelations because at the beginning he never even admitted any justification of new visions. Only the accumulation of his personal and national tragedy made him change his opinion. From the human point of view this was quite understandable, given the pressure of external circumstances and his inner struggle and feeling of hopelessness. His belief in prophecies added a new dimension to Comenius' chiliastic hope – namely confidence that God was still actively intervening in the affairs of humanity and did not abandon true Christians even at times of the greatest trials. This belief gave chiliasm a more concrete content and in extreme situations mobilized the believer to new efforts. In Comenius' thinking it played a key role as an antidote against persistent depressions and, at the same time, as a means of influencing public opinion. His belief in revelations of a better future helped Comenius live in a world filled with hopelessness and spurred his efforts for its reform.

Soon after his arrival in Leszno it did seem that the so fervently desired turn for the better was about to come. In 1630, the Thirty Years' War entered a new stage and after the exhausted Bohemia, the Palatinate, and Denmark, the battle against the Hapsburgs was joined by the Nordic power, Sweden. The Czechs expected much from its king, Gustav Adolf II, whom they associated with the foretold victor over the Catholic Babylon. Gustav Adolf advocated Protestant unity (**Corpus Evangelicorum**), and in the minds of the Czech exiles this fact completely overshadowed the other aspect of his policy, namely territorial conquest and consolidation of Sweden's power position in the north of Europe. The important fact was that the Swedes had gained for some time strategic preponderance in the Holy Roman Empire and that their new ally Saxony invaded Bohemia in the autumn of 1631.

While many exiles quickly returned home, Comenius chose to stay in Leszno where in 1631 and 1632 he feverishly worked on writings concerned with reforms in his liberated country. He realized that it would be impossible simply to revert to the situation as it existed there prior to 1620. The time that had passed since the uprising helped him realize the serious mistakes made by the estates and properly assess the importance of the non-privileged strata of the population, which had spontaneously but most resolutely stood up against the re-Catholization drive of the Hapsburg government after the nobility and the burghers had surrendered. Comenius did not become even now a social revolutionary who would break up the feudal system, but he understood how damaging for the nation had been the insensitivity of the nobles towards their subjects. Therefore, in his book **Haggaeus redivivus** (Haggaeus Resurrected) he appealed to the nobility to treat their subjects fairly and with compassion, to treat them in their own interest „not as cattle but as fellow human beings". The secular nobility and the clergy were to attend to the reconstruction of the country and to furnish it with well organized secular and ecclesiastical administration by overcoming petty differences between the non-Catholics, but especially through a systematic education of the country's youth. The Community of Brethren was to become the core of unification of Czech Protestants and was to prevent subsidiary theological differences obstructing their collaboration in attaining common welfare. Comenius considered as a concrete contribution to a better future the reconstruction and improvement of the schools which were to educate all young people irrespective of their status in society.

The realization of this proposal in a reformed Czech state depended, of course, on success of the anti-Hapsburg coalition. Unfortunately, the Hapsburgs managed to mobilize once again their forces. They returned the title of generalissimus to the outstanding organizer Albrecht of Wallenstein who succeeded in the course of 1632 to push the Saxons out of Bohemia and to stop the Swedish advance in Germany. Moreover, kings Gustav Adolf II and Friedrich of the Palatinate died soon one after the other. This dealt another blow to the Czech exiles who had relied so much on both monarchs. The hope for an early return home once again faded away.

Nevertheless, Comenius still did not abandon his thoughts of an eventual return. He faced the new situation realistically and with still greater energy concentrated on his mission in Leszno. After his arrival there, he first taught at the local superior gymnasium and most probably in 1638 became its director. At the same time he spent much energy working for the Community of Brethren whose synod appointed him in October 1632 one of its bishops with the special authorization as the Community's „scribe". In his new office he was in fact the executive secretary of his church, responsible for literary activities in the interest of the Community and at the same time for supervision over youth preparing for the clerical profession. Although his intentions did not always meet with sufficient understanding in the Community's leadership, in both his ecclesiastical and school offices Comenius found many opportunities to advance systematically his literary and educational projects.

Comenius proceeded from the experience he had gained at schools in Moravia, and continuously expanded it through his teaching practice at the Leszno gymnasium. However, he wanted more than only partial improvement of instruction in different subjects. His objective was theory of instruction in general. His didactical efforts were marked by the constant endeavour to find the way out of the labyrinth of the world he lived in, and education specifically seemed to him to be the appropriate means of attaining a better future. Although he had carefully studied the views of his paedagogical predecessors, he was inspired mainly by the great philosophical concepts of his older contemporaries – the English philosopher Francis Bacon and the Italian Utopian thinker Tomasso Campanella. While Campanella intrigued him by his idea that the subjects taught so far required a thorough reform in order to fit the system of true knowledge, in Bacon he found a more specific directive for this endeavour, namely the accent Bacon placed on a new method of learning, a method that would multiply the forces of the human spirit. These ideas strengthened Comenius' resolve to work out a process which through education would bring about humanity's harmonious development.

Proceeding from the ideological tradition of the Community of Brethren, Comenius searched for a universal order of things, which he reconstructed in ideal form with the help of the syncritical method. This method of learning proceeded from the precept that the universe was organized under common principles; some of them were cognizable through the senses or by reason, while others could be deduced by analogy. This undoubtedly ran counter to the emerging new natural science which, however, suffered from other one-sided premises. Nevertheless, if such presumption of a harmoniously organized universe were indeed valid – and Comenius firmly believed it was – then a comparison of analogical structures parallelly arranged at different levels, necessarily had to produce a harmonious result. Thus, a proper cognition of the foundations should lead to understanding of all things derived from the common principles, and therefore to wisdom. Wisdom, in turn, was to be the means of reforming interhuman relations and of instituting peace and justice. Naturally, in this philosophical perspective education acquired exceptional importance.

The early form of these pansophistic ideas was projected into the Didactics whose Czech manuscript Comenius completed in 1630. In it he explained his philosophy of education as well as the objectives, scope and methods of the educational process. He also worked out the organization of the educational system which was to provide in six-year stages education ranging from the most elementary to the highest; these stages, tying one onto the other began with maternal education (in every family) and then proceeded to elementary, based on the mother tongue (in smaller communities), and secondary based on universal Latin (in larger towns), and the last stage was higher education at academies located in the provincial capitals, which was to be supplemented with travel. The Czech Didactics already reflected the principles of all-round education of all people in all matters essential for life. The educational process was conceived as an entity, covering the period from the earliest age to adulthood, to be based on discipline devoid of force, and aiming at the attainment of good results if possible on the basis of play and joyous concentration and interest.

The Czech Didactics was only one part of Comenius' original concept. He wanted to supplement this theoretical outline with a number of special textbooks for elementary and secondary schools, as well as with instruction books for the educators, i.e. teachers and parents. Of this planned series of books, only the Informatorium of Maternal School, the first book on pre-school education in world paedagogical literature, was completed; Comenius comprehensively analyzed in it questions relating to development of the physical and mental capacity of the smallest children for further education. He was prevented from realizing his other plans by a negative turn of events in Bohemia, which postponed the application of his didactical proposals for a reform of Czech education indefinitely.

Comenius realized already earlier that the tragedy of his country was only part of a great European drama and that it was necessary to strive for a universal reform. After 1632 he therefore addressed his projects mainly to the Protestant world, and in order to make them generally understood, wrote them in Latin. He translated the Czech version of his Didactics into Latin and rewrote it so that it addressed all of Christendom and proposed ways of improving the education of youth in general. This **Didactica magna** (the Great Didactics) offered „the universal art of teaching everybody all, that is a reliable and refined manner whereby schools may be established in all communities, towns and villages, of any Christian kingdom". Comenius rightly considered the Great Didactics to be one of his supreme deeds. However, this work, whose copies he sent to his friends, was not well understood and received, which made its author postpone its publication until 1657.

On the other hand, his textbook of Latin, based on the new didactical methods – **Ianua linguarum reserata** (The Open Gate of Languages) – and first published in 1631, met with instant and unexpected success. In writing it, Comenius proceeded from a criticism of the existing language instruction which was based on reading of classical literature which not only exceeded the perceptive capacity of a child but also offered very little knowledge useful in 17th century life. Discarding memorization of Latin texts and complex theorems, Comenius offered a lively and understandable explanation and interpretation of terms from the fields of inorganic and organic nature, human life, work, culture, ethics, and religion. He fortunately applied his encyclopaedic knowledge and combined instruction of Latin with information about interesting and useful things. This revolutionary method of language instruction perfectly matched the social and cultural requirements of its time and was therefore spontaneously well received not only by Protestants but also by Catholics; in fact, in 1669, while Comenius was still living, it was published by his ideological opponents, the Jesuits of Prague, for their own schools.

The author himself was more critical of his work. When still teaching at Leszno, he realized that his textbook was too difficult for the younger students, and therefore produced an introductory textbook of Latin, **Vestibulum linguarum** (The Antechamber of Languages), which was first published in Leszno in 1633. Moreover, in the subsequent years he also tried to facilitate an active mastery of Latin for the more advanced students by writing school plays on topically presented themes from the Antiquity or the Old Testament. However, his mind was set on completion of a set of textbooks, among which a key role was to be played by a pansophistic encyclopaedia **Ianua rerum** (The Gate of Things). It was conceived as the opposite to the language textbook and its objective was to offer general instruction for an effective choice of the great volume of literature written so far; this selection was to cover all that leads to true wisdom. Comenius wanted to define universally valid criteria which from the pansophistic viewpoint showed the organization and arrangement of all important things, just as the objectives and consequences of everything that was, is or will, or possibly could be. With this design, the philosophy of education was to offer instruction for learning the past, for a critical analysis of the present, and for assessing knowledge for life in the future.

It was thus, that in the shadow of the European renown of his language textbooks, the foundations of the pansophistic work of Comenius were emerging in the 1630s. He made two interlinked attempts to create a philosophical-theoretical system. The first proposed education for all youth up to the age of twenty-four, the second one a set of books for the new concept of school education and for a grandly conceived unification of learning. These projects ensued from a belief in a conflictless interlocking of philosophy and theology, and science and religious faith. In fact, they were influenced by some already then outdated mediaeval ideas about nature and by a lack of understanding of the findings of contemporary exact sciences. That is why they generated polemics and opposition from both mechanistically oriented philosophers and dogmatic theologians who rejected what they claimed was a „demotion" of theology. The positive, activating and reform elements of Comenius' projects had to wait for their appreciation until the centuries to come.

Nevertheless, his pansophistic ideas did meet with a positive response also among Comenius' contemporaries who believed in the possibility of reforming the turbulent world. The strongest response came from a country which stood at the threshold of a bourgeois revolution – from distant England. There, a group of intellectuals knew some of Comenius' Latin works and turned their attention to him especially after his book **Conatuum Comenianorum praeludia** (Preludes to Comenius' Endeavours) had been published at Oxford in 1637. This group of „Comenians" offered Comenius to participate in a project of improving English schools and science, and invited him to London. Thus, new prospects emerged for Comenius at the threshold of his fiftieth year.

A Servant of His Nation
in Service of Humanity

In the midst of the universal destruction brought upon the nations of Europe by the Thirty Years'War in the 1630s, voices were increasingly heard, calling for a turn in the dismal situation. Not merely by ending the slaughter on and off the battlefields, but through a far-reaching reform of society. This involved a thorough elimination of the causes that produced wars, as well as of the hostility between states, nations, and different religious faiths. These reform projects featured two main objectives for the nearest future. The first one was the unification of the Protestant churches, which should have first ensured joint action by the Protestants against the re-Catholization offensive, then completion of the reformation process, and finally the institution of a lasting religious peace. The second objective was to be an educational reform which should have raised the cultural standard of the European nations and promoted their mutual understanding.

The advocates of these reform projects did not stay confined to their cabinets, but tried to establish closer mutual contacts and win other adherents, especially those with political influence. One of these prominent reform thinkers, who was a skilful organizer of written and personal contacts among them, was Samuel Hartlib, a German scholar from the Baltic town of Elblag, who thanks to his English mother had a special affinity for England where he eventually settled in 1628. Another resident of Elblag, which had a significant colony of English merchants, was the Scottish preacher John Dury who became Hartlib's friend and eagerly promoted his projects. While Hartlib concentrated on the reform of education and science, Dury's primary interest was a peaceful reconciliation of the Protestants. Both where well acquainted with the situation on the European continent and at the same time had a close relationship to England which, they felt, was best suited as a base and centre for the reform efforts. The two men also shared the view that the most promising ideas for a reform of the people of Europe were to be found in the pansophistic works of Comenius. Therefore, Hartlib arranged the publication of Comenius' works in England between 1637 and 1639, and tried to expand the circle of his adherents. He succeeded in rallying around himself several intellectuals who expressly championed Comenius' pansophistic ideas. They even believed that Comenius had been sent to the Earth from the heavens in order to help the confused humanity. This Comenian Group was so assertive, that the English historian H. R. Trevor-Roper described its representatives, headed by Comenius' as the ideologues of the English revolution. Although this overrated characterization has not been universally accepted, it is a fact that at the beginning of the 1640s the Comenian Group enjoyed the favour of many influential personalities in the English Parliament and that this new situation offered Comenius during his stay in London unexpected prospects.

Comenius shared the view that England was the country best suited for launching the pansophistic reform. It had been spared until then the disastrous impact of the Thirty Years' War, it had good maritime links with the rest of the world, and its economic and political influence was rapidly rising. Moreover, the local intelligentsia respected the philosophical heritage of Francis Bacon, which had also been embraced by the Czech thinker. Comenius' name was mentioned in the English Parliament still before his arrival in London, when at the end of 1640, that body was addressed in the spirit of the Comenian efforts by the preacher John Gauden who praised the work whereby Comenius – as he said – had laid the foundations and a lovely outline for erecting a structure truly human and divine, most useful to all of humankind for a facile understanding of things. Gauden at the same time urged the parliament to invite Comenius and Dury to England at the earliest date and to provide them with material assistance the realization of their noble designs.

Although the invitation eventually came not from the parliament as a whole but only from a group of interested individuals, Comenius was full of optimism when he arrived in London in September 1641. He believed he would gain financial support for the exiled members of the Community of Brethren and that his work would help internationalize once again the Czech question, especially if England joined the anti-Hapsburg coalition. As far as his work was concerned, it was especially important that for the first time he had the opportunity to realize his pansophistic ideas and his educational reforms. The „Long Parliament" then in session was discussing questions of church and political reform, and thus the proposals offered by Comenius and the Comenian Group came at a propitious time. Serious interest in them was shown by the Anglican Church hierarchy, many members of the moderate opposition, and even John Pym, the leader of the revolutionary parliament between 1641 and 1643. The material aspects of the situation were also favourable because in the summer of 1641, the parliament decided that part of the confiscated church property should be used for assisting scholarly endeavours.

As early as in October 1641, Comenius addressed the English public with two writings in which he outlined his plans. He proposed a reform of education and the schools, and explained his ideas about the way to reconciliation of the churches and to universal peace. At the same time he specified the tasks whereby he wanted to attain his goal; they included mainly the publication of the necessary books which he would himself write or edit, promotion of the school reform, organization of the necessary work and mutual consultations, and collection of funds for financing all the reform activities. It seemed that the institutionalization of these projects was at hand. Parliament wanted to provide the Comenians with a financially endowed college where a team of scholars was to work on and direct the reform of education and science. Comenius' friends urged him to assume the leadership of such team and to settle with his family permanently in London. Comenius realized that he would hardly find such favourable conditions elsewhere and was prepared to accept the offer. However, he asked the leadership of the Community and Brethren and, of course, his wife for their consent. While his colleagues were rather vague in their response, his wife Marie Dorota Komenská resolutely refused to move to a distant, unknown country, reminded her husband of his duties as bishop towards the exiles settled in Leszno, and pleaded with him to think of the approaching death. However, Comenius was at the peak of his energy and would have probably continued striving for the realization of his pansophistic dream, had the situation in England not taken a drastic turn.

At the beginning of November 1641, reports reached London about the uprising of Catholic Ireland against the English rule, and speeded up the polarization of political forces. Under the pressure of these events, the patrons of the Comenian Group split to join the hostile camps of the royalists and the revolutionary parliament. Comenius, who did not speak English, was unable to understand fully the essence of the social upheaval, but he realized that the crisis shattered the recently so promising expectations. Although his friends promised him that once peace was restored, they would return to their reform efforts, but could not offer him any security for the nearest future. Thus, in the winter months of 1641 and 1642, Comenius had no other option left but to return to the Continent. He parted with England in a most dignified manner and dedicated to his friends and patrons his work **Via lucis** (The Way of Light).

In this work Comenius symbolically depicted the eternal struggle between the good and wisdom on one side and the evil and ignorance on the other side, expressing these concepts with the symbols of light and darkness. He conceived the growth of civilization in the form of stages, the youngest of which – bookprinting and maritime navigation – he praised as a tremendous enrichment of humanity with new possibilities of communication. But now, in the middle of the 17th century – he said – the human community faced the task of attaining true wisdom as the precondition for peace and universal welfare. In order to accomplish this goal, it was essential to fulfil four conditions – produce universally valid books, create a general school for all youth, establish a universal advisory body, and create a universal language in which the words would exactly express their objects and which would ensure perfect understanding. These projects for the first time reflected the concept of pansophy as means of universal reform, which Comenius further elaborated for the rest of his life.

An idea of special significance, which tied onto the Comenians' debates that helped form the ideological model of the **Via lucis**, as well as onto older concepts, was that of an international college. This world organization of scholars was to associate pansophically-oriented researchers and guide them towards work on pansophistic books and towards realization of common, humanity-wide ideals. The chairman of this „assembly of light" was to reside in London and on the basis of reports from scholars in different countries on progress made in the pansophic efforts and on the course of public affairs in those countries, he was to draw up a comprehensive annual report and send it to all countries, and thereby, in return, guide the activities of the collaborating scholars. Their special task was to strive in their respective countries for a uniform system of schools, based on the principles of pansophy. This idea of regular collaboration of scholars, financed from public funds, of their purposeful ties and activities guided by the same spirit for understanding among nations, documented a new concept of intellectual activity and joint responsibility of spiritual workers for the emancipation of their own nations as well as of all humanity.

Comenius' pansophic thinking matured in this particular book into its first comprehensive shape and provided its author the basis for his further efforts for universal reform. However, it also influenced the cultural development of the host country which, proceeding from the Comenians' suggestions, established the Royal Society in 1662. It was to this institution that Comenius dedicated his **Via lucis** when he published it a quarter of a century after he had written it for the first time in print in Amsterdam in 1668.

The civil war in England was yet another of Comenius' many frustrations and disappointments. Nevertheless, in spite of his serious reservations he had towards the radical Independents, he did not break off his contacts with revolutionary England. As he was leaving London in June 1642, he was already determined not to accept an invitation from France's First Minister, Cardinal Richelieu, to come to Paris. He preferred the Nordic big power, Sweden, to the anti-Hapsburg but Catholic France. Therefore, he accepted an invitation from the Dutch-Swedish merchant and arms manufacturer Louis de Geer to take part in preparations for a reform of Swedish schools.

It was on his journey through the Netherlands in July 1642, when Comenius had his memorable meeting with the French philosopher René Descartes who a year earlier had published his principal work, **Meditationes de prima philosophia** (Meditations About First Philosophy). Their four-hour conversation at Endegeest manor near Leiden was a confrontation of two basically different views of the world. While Comenius defended a link between science and faith, Descartes denied the authority of the Bible in his philosophical considerations. In his approach to nature, he was undoubtedly less influenced by tradition and showed greater consistency in concentrating on a mechanistically understood movement of matter. He proceeded from the optimism of natural science and from the idea that everything may be expressed in quantitative terms. Next to him, Comenius appeared old-fashioned and his thinking was burdened by Biblical authorities, mysticism, and mediaeval scholasticism. However, in contrast to Descartes, who exactly grasped and depicted partial natural phenomena, Comenius retained his sense of the comprehensivenes of nature, of the dynamics of history, and of the creative character of the human being. When the two scholars parted – politely but coolly – a wall of mutual lack of understanding remained between them. Comenius felt uneasy about the consequences of Descartes' philosophy. His concern was justified because while Cartesianism opened the door to modern, technological civilization, it deprived man of his human qualities and turned him into a component of a rigid world that could be expressed by mathematical formulas.

Comenius had certainly no intention of abandoning his pansophist plans and hoped that he could further develop them in Sweden which dominated northern Europe and was still at war with the Austrian Hapsburgs. It was precisely from Lutheran Sweden that Comenius expected substantial support for the defeated Czech nation, and filled with new hope set out to negotiate with Queen Kristina and her Chancellor Axel Oxenstierna, the man who shaped Swedish foreign policy. They both showed understanding for his pleas for assistance because the Swedish offensive then under way in Moravia and Silesia warranted their hope that they would decide on the future form of Central European affairs.

For a Czech Brother who was close to Calvinism, strictly Lutheran Sweden was not the ideal place of work. That is why in the period 1642 – 1648 he settled with his family in Elblag on the east coast of the Baltic Sea, which was within the Swedish sphere of influence. His new patron Louis de Geer had not much understanding for universal pansophist ideas, but in his pronounced practicism he was seriously interested in new textbooks for Swedish schools. Comenius therefore once again set out to modify and improve his philological handbooks and explained his pioneering concept of instruction in the book **Methodus linguarum novissima** (The Latest Language Method). However, he continued to consider his main task to be pansophist studies and their expansion with the objective of a universal reform. It was in Elblag – probably in 1644 – where Comenius began his most grandiose work, **De rerum humanarum emendatione consultatio catholica** (General Discourse on Reform of Human Affairs) in which pansophy was gradually included as only one of seven basic parts.

The General Discourse was taking shape in a whirlpool of events which for a time encouraged Comenius' hopes that he might live to see the first practical steps towards a reform of human society. This was due to the fact that under the reign of the Polish king Władysław IV, Polish Protestants, who had been split into a number of small churches, showed an inclination towards better mutual understanding and unification, and also considered the possibility of reconciliation talks with the Catholics. Comenius joined these negotiations with great enthusiasm for ecumenical understanding between different confessions, but soon ran into insurmountable obstacles. The **Colloquium charitativum** at Toruń, in which he had placed great expectations, collapsed in 1645 in a clash of irreconcilable positions held by the Lutherans and the Jesuits, incited in their hostility also from abroad. The Swedish government viewed these negotiations as subversive, as directed against Lutheranism as well as against its own expansive goals, and saw Comenius' participation in the negotiations almost as treason. When he travelled to Stockholm in 1646, Comenius found that Chancellor Oxenstierna's attitude towards himself and the cause of the Czech exiles had greatly cooled off. Louis de Geer was not fully satisfied with Comenius' work of the textbooks either. Comenius tried to stem the growing tension in his relations with his Swedish patrons by returning to Leszno where in the summer of 1648 he assumed the office of the leading bishop of the Community of Brethren.

Already before then, Comenius was fully preoccupied by the course of the peace congress in the Westphalian towns of Münster and Osnabrück. He bore constantly in mind the Czech question and its favourable settlement, and therefore went to North Germany in 1647 to remind the German Protestants of the fate of their Czech coreligionists. However, he met with the same negative result as in his subsequent interventions with Chancellor Oxenstierna. In his confrontation with realistically-thinking politicians who pursued their specific power interests, he could not use other but ethical and religious arguments. He defended the general ideas of Protestantism and within this framework demanded restoration of the religious and political situation in the lands of the Czech Crown, as it existed in 1618. As the idealist he was, he could not acquiesce with the downright practicism and selfishness of the diplomats, nor was he fully aware of the profound changes that had taken place in his country. Having been separated so long from his native land, he did not realize how much the Hapsburgs had consolidated their power in Bohemia and Moravia during his exile and how far the process of re-Catholization of the ruling strata of the population had advanced; he failed to grasp the fact that two generations had grown up there, who viewed the course of events differently from the Community exiles. It was these very people who took up arms to defend their bare existence and in the hope of ending the Thirty Years' War repelled Swedish attacks on Prague and Brno. The Swedish and German Lutheran diplomats accepted this situation and thus also restoration on the conditions in the Hapsburg monarchy as they existed in 1624, that is the conditions instituted by the victorious Hapsburgs after the battle on White Mountain. For Comenius and the Czech exiles this was a crushing defeat.

Comenius reacted to reports about the conclusion of the Peace of Westphalia with a letter he addressed to Chancellor Oxenstierna on October 11, 1648. Speaking on behalf of the exiled part of his defeated nation, he desperately cried: „I beseech you to look at this nation which was the first among the nations of Europe, which Jesus Christ so graciously chose to lift from the darkness of Antichrist, the nation which earlier than others had accepted enlightenment, which for an entire century had alone withstood the frenzied rage of Antichrist. And recently, when the enemies decided to uproot all, one after the other, our nation was the first that stemmed the onslaught and by its own destruction gave the others the opportunity to defend themselves." However, the reference to the Hussite revolution which presaged the European Reformation, and to the Czech anti-Hapsburg uprising which started the Thirty Years' War, sounded in the middle of the 17th century as a mere echo of a past long gone. Europe faced other problems and lost all interest in the Czech question.

For Comenius, 1648 was not only a year marked by the unjust Peace of Westphalia, but also a year of personal tragedy the death of his second wife who had shared with him twenty-four years of his hard life and bore him four children, the youngest of whom, Daniel, was only two years old. It was mainly his concern about the small boy, that made Comenius soon marry his third wife, Jana Gajusová, the daughter of a Czech Protestant pastor. At that time, Comenius' elder daughters were reaching adulthood and one of them, Alžběta, married, shortly after her father's own marriage in 1649, his loyal collaborator Petr Figulus-Jablonský. Their children, among whom the most outstanding was Daniel Arnošt Jablonský, bishop of the Community of Brethren and co-founder of the Berlin Academy, ensured the continuation of Comenius' family along the female line until the 20th century.

However, Comenius could not enjoy his grandchildren. He went through a period of utter disenchantment and scepticism. After the international recognition of the re-Catholization of the Czech lands, he even felt doubt for some time about the future of his own church which had been greatly weakened and existed scattered in isolated groups in distant European countries. He parted with the church to which he tended his whole life in his touching Testament of the Dying Mother of the Community of Brethren; he bequeathed the Community's heritage to other Protestant churches and pleaded with them for their mutual understanding and unity. With captivating artistic power he expressed his undying love of his country, language and nation which was to become the bearer of the Community's cultural heritage. His visionary words – „I, too, trust the Almighty that once the tempest of wrath has passed . . . thy sovereign rule shall return to thee, my Czech people!" – became a rallying call for the Czech nation, that added strength to it until its restored independence.

In 1650, when the Testament was published in Leszno, the local synod decided that the Community would not be dissolved. Comenius was chosen to continue carrying the burden of maintaining its existence. He was to seek new allies who would help the Brethren survive their exile and perhaps even return to their homeland. The anti-Hapsburg forces were then focussing their attention on the Princedom of Transylvania, a butter state in the borderland between the Hapsburg realm and the Ottoman empire, and hoped that the conflict with France, Transylvania, and other European powers could eventually force the Hapsburgs to make some concessions. With these considerations in mind and impressed by political prophecies which foretold the Transylvanian princely dynasty of the Rákoczis success in the fight against „Antichrist", Comenius decided to move from Leszno to the Rákoczi's residential town of Sárospatak where he was offered the opportunity to reform the local school and apply in it his pansophic system. However, in the backward, feudal situation prevailing in Transylvania, he did not find favourable conditions for doing so. In spite of all his efforts, he only succeeded in reforming the study of Latin in several classes, which was adjusted to his language textbooks.

Comenius apply made up for the unsuccessful practical results of his educational work at Sárospatak by intensive literary work. He wrote several dozen smaller and large books. Some of them elaborated his theory of a pansophic school (**Schola pansophica**) and concept of culture (**De cultura ingeniorum** – Cultivation of the Spirit), while others improved school instruction through greater demonstrativeness, such as **Orbis sensualium pictus** (The World in Pictures), or by using dramatic forms, such as those described in his book **Schola ludus** (School on the Stage). In particular the two latter books, published in print in the period 1656 – 1658, further enhanced Comenius' fame as the foremost educator of the times.

However, in Sárospatak proper, Comenius ran into a lack of understanding on the part of his colleagues and even into hostility on the part of the

Hungarian independents whose teachings he publicly denounced as a source of chaos in society. Comenius' expectations about the role the Rákoczis could play in the anti-Hapsburg coalition failed to materialize either. Although in June 1651, Prince Sigismund Rákoczi married the daughter of the Czech ex-king Friedrich of the Palatinate, Henrietta Marie, and Comenius himself blessed the marriage, the premature death of the newlyweds frustrated this alliance by marriage. Comenius realized that in Transylvania he could not assert his intentions in either the political or the pansophic spheres, and parted with the host country in 1654 with his book **Gentis felicitas** (The Happiness of a Nation). In it he proposed profound internal reforms in Transylvania and at the same offered a remarkably formulated general theory of a nation, which is surprisingly close to the views held in the 20th century.

Comenius' return to his third and last stay in Leszno (1654 – 1656) was marked by a deep crisis of the Polish kingdom and its battle for its very existence. At the time when Poland was weakened by its war with Russia, it was invaded by the Swedish army which occupied a large part of the country. Comenius had friendly feelings towards the Poles and considered Poland to be his second homeland, but in this case, when the country was threatened by division and foreign occupation, he failed to realize that a Swedish victory would mean for the Poles an even greater disaster that the defeat on White Mountain was for the Czechs. He saw the Swedes mainly as Protestants and expected from them internal reforms and institution of religious freedom. This was also the spirit of his eulogy of the Swedish king Karl Gustav X, which was later mistakenly viewed as an anti-Polish pamphlet. However, once again political developments disproved Comenius' expectations. A popular uprising and guerilla warfare helped push the Swedes out of Poland. In the course of the fighting, the Polish, Catholic-oriented troops occupied Leszno and burned it to the ground as a „nest of heretics". Although Comenius and his family saved their life and a few unpublished manuscripts, he lost in the flames of Leszno at the end of April 1656 all his property, including his library and many unfinished manuscripts. Among others, the flames engulfed the final drafts of his pansophic works, his sermons, and the Treasury of the Czech Language, to which he had devoted thirty years of his life.

Thus, at the age of sixty-four, Comenius again found himself practically penniless. During a brief sojourn in Silesia where the exiles from Leszno escaped in utmost distress, he moved with his family from one place to another because like all the exiles he felt threatened both by the Polish troops and the Hapsburg authorities. Comenius found it most difficult to reconcile himself with the irreparable loss of his works, but soon his creative spirit and indomitable desire for literary activity once again prevailed: „Whatever may happen, if this endless dissipation of my mind so permits, I desire to compose a picture of this disaster." This is what Comenius wrote in conclusion of a tragic balance sheet of his losses on May 22, 1656. He supplemented it with a request that his son-in-law, Petr Figulus, notify his old friends and patrons of his misfortune. He listed in first place Laurens de Geer, the son of his patron of many years ago.

It was Laurens de Geer, too, who invited Comenius to come to Amsterdam in order to spend there the rest of his life in safety. Comenius thus left for the metropolis he called the „glory of cities, the jewel of the Netherlands, and the pride of Europe". He went far away from his vanquished and oppressed country in order to expand his work and to address it to all of humanity.

The Messenger of Peace

„Finally, after many adversities and events I have reached Amsterdam. Here then I am, where the force of destiny has brought me, but among friends and supporters who have kindly received me. Especially the benefactor who has been encouraging my pansophic studies for twelve years already and has not ceased being most gracious and generous to me, so that I am beginning to recover. I may say: We are well being here . . ." This is how Comenius announced his arrival in the Netherlands to one of his friends early in September 1656, at a time when he regained his balance. He thought of the ancient Roman poet Publius Terentius who, after his works had been destroyed, died of sorrow, and praised God for the gift of patience granted to him, thanks to which he had been able to bear alone this latest trial. However, it was not a passive acceptance of fate, which gave Comenius his strength, but his indomitable belief in the mission he was yet to accomplish.

After a life spent mostly in small, provincial towns, at the threshold of old age Comenius found himself in one of the busies metropolises of Western Europe. With its roughly 150,000 inhabitants, Amsterdam led the United Provinces of the Low Countries and brilliantly represented the economic prosperity, political self-assurance, and high cultural ambitions of the victorious burghers. This environment, full of intellectual ferment, could hardly become a peaceful resting place for the perceptive immigrant. It did, however, offer favourable conditions for the application of his creative energy and interests in many areas. It was not only his „most gracious benefactor", the rich praised merchant and dedicated supporter of pansophic efforts, Laurens de Geer, who provided the Czech scholar and his family with lodging and material security, that stood behind the new upsurge of Comenius' activities. There were also other friends, among them mainly the Calvinist pastor Johannes Rulitius who arranged for Comenius' contacts with the all-powerful city council. However, Comenius was already such a well known personality of European science, that the elders of Amsterdam received him with respect and immediately offered him unusually generous assistance. The city granted him honorary professorship at the Gymnasium Illustre, known as Athenaeum, which became the foundation of the subsequent Amsterdam University. At the same time, the city council provided a grant for the publication of already completed didactic works. Similar contacts with Comenius were established by the synod of the Amsterdam Reformed Church. Comenius reported to them on the difficult situation of the Protestants who remained in Poland after the burning of Leszno, and acquired for them considerable financial assistance as a token of solidarity of the Dutch people with their corcligionists in Central Europe.

Thus, Comenius once again entered public life. It is not certain whether besides his literary work he was also involved in practical instruction. But he did devote much of his energy to the administration of his church and to publication of books for the Community of Brethren. For this purpose he even set up a printing shop employing two Czech exiles, and in order to meet legal requirements, he himself joined the guild of Amsterdam printers. However these official negotiations and administrative duties were not his only worries. In his advanced age, he found burdensome frequent visits by scholars and student from abroad, who came to Amsterdam to seek advice from Comenius or simply wanted to meet the famous man personally. Comenius could never turn down these visits, but often felt extremely tured. „Am I, perhaps, the Atlas whose shoulders should bear all the mountains of even foreign burdens?", he asked himself in one of his letters. And for this reason he did not refuse the offer of the noble Laurens de Geer to spend some time in his rural residence in order to concentrate at least temporarily on literary work.

The results of Comenius' stay in Amsterdam, especially its first half, were truly impressive. In terms of the number of published books, that period represented the culmination of Comenius' entire work, and some of the earlier grand projects were completed as well. A truly grandiose project was the **Opera didactica omnia**, Comenius' assembled didactical works, which was published by the Amsterdam city council with the date 1657 early in 1658. This was not simply a new edition of older works on education, but a specially conceived complex of works, which documented Comenius' quest for the best educational method and at the same time its concrete results. The author arranged his works in chronological order and divided them into four parts of which every part covered one of the principal periods of his work. These periods were linked with his sojourns in Leszno, Elblag, Sárospatak, and finally in Amsterdam. In each of these parts Comenius first offered a paedagogical and didactical explanation on the theoretical level and then demonstrated the practical realization of the outlined objectives in the form of textbooks and handbooks.

Comenius pointed the way to perfection of the instruction by an ever more precise realization of analogical educational objectives. At the same time, he explained his process within the framework of objective historical circumstances as well as of his own intellectual growth, and thereby most plastically produced his intellectual autobiography. He published there for the first time his older major work, **Didactica magna**, and the Latin version of his Czech and German handbook on pre-school education, **Schola infantiae**. The fourth part of **Opera**, which contained Comenius' works from the period 1654 – 1657, met demands for a summary of the most essential principles of the paedagogical work of the great man. He outlined these principles in a form which made them understandable also to those who had not read the whole collection.

The author explained his method of instruction in the treatise **E scholasticis labyrinthis exitus in planum** (The Way out of the Schools' Labyrinths). There he returned to the manneristic idea of the Labyrinth, which had accompanied him since his youth, and critically assessed the existing schools; they appeared to him chaotic precisely because they had no clear objective and the less so the means of attaining it. He himself recommended a procedure which would meet human nature and the pupil's abilities. The pupil should form his opinion through sensual cognition, obtain practical habits by his own actions and behaviour, and attain proper utilization of the acquired knowledge through understanding of its superior goal. Comenius' idea of reform was thus of creating such a form of education, that would produce an understanding of things, result in practical activity, and help proper communication between people.

Comenius explained his theoretical principles immediately in subsequent treatises in which he proposed what concrete measures should be taken. His **Latium redivivum** (Latium Resurrected) outlined for the Amsterdam city council the project of a model Latin school which Comenius thought about already at Sárospatak, but now, the situation in an advanced Western metropolis seemed to him much more favourable for its establishment. **Typographaeum vivum** (Living Printshop) compared the school to a printing shop in that the school should impress knowledge into the soul of every pupil with such clarity as the printing press does on the paper. Finally, his **Paradisus juventuti christianae reducendus** (Paradise Restored to Christian Youth) underlined the objective of school education and its ties to pansophy. Even after having collected and re-assessed all his didactical works, Comenius felt that the road to improving the education of youth remained open, and in his didactical testament, **Traditio lampadis** (Passing the Torch), he addressed a message to all his successors. However, not even at this moment would he let the long-term prospects overshadow the practical application of the knowledge and findings obtained so far. He addressed a proposal to „the wise City Council of Amsterdam" for the creation of a didactical college which would put into effect the findings assembled in his **Opera didactica omnia.**

Comenius preserved his remarkable sense for a live contact with social practice even after the publication of his didactical works, which raised his international reputation and authority to its zenith. In his writings he tried to respond to all ideas and to express his views on a wide range of political, philosophical, and religious problems of those days. Such frequent polemics demonstrated his remarkable vitality, but brought him much disappointment and detracted him from the realization of the main task that arose for him in Amsterdam. Shortly after Comenius' arrival in the Netherlands, Laurens de Geer read two volumes of **Consultatio catholica**, the work about universal reform of humanity, and had them printed. Comenius' other friends and patrons, just like de Geer, impatiently waited for the completion of the great book about universal reform. Although Comenius did not forget his **Consultatio** and whenever possible worked on it, other ideas and subsidiary interests constantly swayed his attention in other directions.

In his late sixties, Comenius managed to accomplish work that would have kept several diligent scholars busy. By publishing additional textbooks he complemented his past theoretical work and strengthened his international reputation as educator; the popularity of his language textbooks was such, that the university at Leiden even considered the publication of **Ianua linguarum** in five Oriental languages – Arabic, Turkish, Persian, Tatar, and Armenian. Another sphere of his activities, the publication of religious books in Czech, Polish, and German, was important for adding spiritual strength to the thinning ranks of his coreligionists from the Community of Brethren. But he also considered broader missionary projects, among them in particular concrete negotiations on translation of the Bible into Turkish, which ensued from Comenius' irenic ideas and from an effort to bridge the religious and political conflicts between Christians and Muslims.

Much less promising was his effort to delve into the mysteries of physics and mechanics, which were obviously beyond the range of his deeper understanding. Nevertheless, he did engage in a sharp polemic directed against Descartes' natural philosophy, and in 1659 published a treatise in which he described the spreading Cartesianism as „the most malignant of all philosophies" and as a haven of the godless. He was as uncompromising in his polemic with the Socinians who in their reform radicalism denied the Christian dogma of the Trinity. Denial of Christ's divinity was utterly unacceptable for Comenius since his early youth, when he had passed through a doctrinal crisis, because he linked his hope for an eventual reform of all humanity precisely with the chiliastic belief in an early coming of the kingdom of Jesus Christ.

Paradoxically, the polemic with the Socinians brought Protestants and Catholics closer together, and Comenius had entered it already at an earlier date. However, in the late 1650s and early 1660s, the tragedy of mutual misunderstanding was the greater as it included a sharp clash between representatives of the Czech Community of Brethren and of the Polish Brethren, who tended towards Socinianism, i. e. between two movements which were suppressed by the Catholics in both Bohemia and Moravia, and whose members had found refuge in the tolerant Netherlands. At that time Comenius wrote three polemic treatises against Daniel Zwicker, a former physician in Gdańsk, who was also living in exile in the Netherlands. Comenius, just as Zwicker, desired universal peace, but each of them saw the dogmatic foundation of his irenism in what his opponent could not accept. Both claimed that they were using rational arguments and were proceeding from a proper interpretation of the Bible, but in fact they distance between them was steadily growing. More was already involved than verbal misunderstanding, for in his polemical zeal, Comenius did not stop at disproval of Socinian thesis and at denouncing Zwicker as a heretic, but went as far as calling on Dutch Calvinist theologians to help him silence Zwicker.

Some of his friends rightly thought that Comenius was unnecessarily wasting his waning energy, and Samuel Hartlib quite openly expressed his opinion that Comenius would do better to ignore the Socinians and to continue working on his pansophic writings. However, for Comenius the chiliastic prospect was a key question which he was unable to avoid in silence. Moreover, he was being detracted from his emendatory work by additional problems, among which a dispute about revelations and their place in the contemporary political events occupied a prominent place.

This international polemic about revelations was sparked by Comenius when he published **Lux in tenebris** (Light in Darkness) in Amsterdam in 1657. In this book he assembled in Latin translation and with his own political interpretation prophecies of Christoph Kotter, a Silesian, Kristina Poniatowska, a Czech woman of Polish origin, and, more recently, of the Moravian Mikuláš Drabík. He was especially attracted by the prophecies of Drabík, a priest of the Community, once Comenius' fellow-student, and now an exile in Hungary. Drabík's prophecies expressed the unwarranted hopes of the Czech exiles for a defeat of the Hapsburgs and their own return home, but too transparently linked them to the current activity of the European powers, mainly France, Sweden, and Transylvania. Although Drabík had rightly foretold the death of Emperor Ferdinand III in 1657, his deduction were otherwise far removed from political reality. Quite absurd were his assumptions that the Turks would convert to Christianity and help the Protestants in fighting the Hapsburg Antichrist. While the Turkish armies soon did penetrate deep into the Hapsburg realm, the expected effects did not materialize. On the contrary, the merciless plunder which during the war also seriously affected Moravia in 1663 still further deepened the enmity between the Christian population and the Osman invaders.

The response to the prophecies in Western Europe was contradictory. Comenius' uncritical belief in these new revelations was shared only by his English friends who also combined social Utopias with chiliasm and mysticism. In the Netherlands, on the other hand, some theologians resolutely opposed the prophecies and refused to compare them to Biblical revelations. Suspicion even arose that some of the prophecies were invented by Comenius himself in order to influence European public opinion. He deemed it essential to defend his integrity and the truthfulness of the published prophecies in his **Historia revelationum** (A History of Revelations), printed in 1659. However, the arguments he used did not convince many readers, and soon thereafter his once pupil Nicolas Arnoldus criticized Comenius. He uncompromisingly rejected the prophecies published and advocated by his former teacher as a confused compound of divine and human affairs, and accused Comenius of incitement to war and of tending towards atheism.

His unorthodox religious opinions had brought Comenius already earlier to disputes with his coreligionists from the Community of Brethren, but now he entered into protracted theological polemics which filled the last decade of his life. His advocacy of the revelations was encouraged by general feeling of insecurity, generated by the Turkish offensive in the east and an epidemic of the plague in the west of Europe, which in Amsterdam alone killed more than 30, 000 people in 1663 and 1664. In this high-strung mood, Comenius sent copies of the revelations to many European countries, from England to the Turkish empire, and wrote the admonishment **Letzte Posaun über Deutschland** (The Last Trombone Over Germany) in 1663, in which he presented in the spirit of 16th century opinion the Turkish threat as the whip of God which by strict punishment should lead corrupt Christendom to reform. He also compiled an enlarged collection of prophecies **Lux e tenebris** (Light from Darkness) and published it at Leiden in 1665. The polemic about revelations continued and culminated in 1669 – 1670 in a sharp clash with the French theologian Samuel Maresius, who was a professor at the university in Groningen. This militant Calvinist rejected belief in revelations as well as chiliasm as the keystone of Comenius' reform efforts. From this orthodox viewpoint, Comenius appeared as a bad theologian, and his efforts to reconcile members of different religious denominations were condemned as improper delusion. The aggressively personal tenor of the polemic made Comenius write an apologia in the form of his autobiography which was the only valuable product of his last painful disoute. Generally, however, this sharp exchange of opinion showed the complexity of the situation in which Comenius' reform endeavours were being born, and indicated how difficult it would be to assert the desire for humanity at peace not only in the 17th century but in the distant future as well.

In the last years of his life, Comenius completed in a dramatic inner struggle his image of humanity's road to peace. This Czech thinker's development was not straightforward and he did not arrive at the usual Utopia of an ideal world devoid of wars. He was too well aware of the existing impoverished state of interhuman and international relations not to be able to ignore it. Nor could he forget his own shocking experiences, or the feeling that he was being constantly pursued by the unleashed monster of war. For he himself had been so often a victim of the horrors of war, driven by them from one place to another, over and over again! His early childhood was marked by the invasion of Moravia by Hungarian rebels and by the devastation of his native region. And then came the endless raging of the Thirty Years and the Swedish-Polish Wars which killed his family and friends and turned his writings into ashes. As a homeless person he fled from Fulnek and then from Leszno, fearing the distant Turkish threat as well as the closer Hapsburg power. He perceived the danger of aggressive Islam as well as of irreconcilable, militant Catholicism, which he had to face as a member and later one of the leaders of the politically powerless Community of Brethren.

In his immense desire for an active deed, Comenius many times tied his hopes for the liberation of his country to anti-Hapsburg coalitions. In 1654 he even stood in the background of a project according to which the Czech exiles, with the help of revolutionary England and Oliver Cromwell personally, were to invade Bohemia and there institute religious freedom. However, all such military plans, whether close to political reality, or merely wishful thinking, failed in the end. If Comenius were not to fall into utter despair, he had to find other solutions. In this desperate search he found encouragement in political prophecies whose practical value rested in the possibility Comenius found in them to formulate his own opinion and publicize it. However, as the publisher and the interpreter of these prophecies he had to present his own opinion which changed and matured in the course of time. As late as in the 1657 edition of the revelations his commentary sounded quite militant. For him the corruption of the world was symbolized by the papacy and the Hapsburg power. Both were to be destroyed and washed away in a deluge of blood. Eight years later the world appeared different to him. He did not want to condemn or insult either Emperor Leopold I or Pope Alexander VII. On the contrary, it was to them that he addressed in 1665 his **Lux e tenebris**, urging them to repent and to reform on the basis of an understanding of their own errors. Other addressees included the rulers of Europe and especially the French king Louis XIV who was to convene a general Christian council and there help a settlement of religious and political conflicts. Under this concept, the revelations no longer encouraged wars, but their end, just as the end of religious persecution, and a settlement of public affairs in the spirit of the Gospel, that is universal justice.

Comenius believed that an opportunity to assert these principles in international relations was offered by the peace congress which met in Breda in 1667. Its purpose was to end the second, rather inconclusive war between England and the Netherlands for trading privileges, colonies, and domination of the seas. Comenius addressed to the diplomats of both sides the appeal **Angelus pacis** (The Messenger of Peace) and at the age of seventy-five personally went to Breda. He had serious grounds for attaching such exceptional significance to the Breda congress. By then he had already reached the point where he envisioned Europe as an equitable system of states, from which he did not exclude either the Muslim Turks or the Catholics, including the Hapsburg and the Jesuits; in fact, he was considering the possibility of winning the collaboration of the Society of Jesus in the manuscript of **Clamores Eliae** (The Pleadings of Elijah) on which he was then working. The hub of this system was to be formed, naturally, by the Protestant countries and among them in particular the two greatest naval powers. Seen from this vantage point, the peace talks between England and the Netherlands appeared to Comenius not only as a means of ending a war, but also as a starting point of a reform of international relations. Comenius wanted to serve the reform with his entire work and offered to the negotiating diplomats those of his writings which formulated the fundamental principles of an equitable and just world system. These principles included a reconciliation of the churches on the basis of broad tolerance, creation of new international institutions, and regulation of the policy pursued by the European states in the chiliastic spirit.

Comenius – the Messenger of Peace – addressed the negotiating countries with concrete proposals which were to launch the process of reform. He appealed to the English, the Dutch, just as the French and the Swedes, to conclude an alliance and jointly defend freedom for all, because such coalition would be indomitable. Comenius remained aloof from their contradictory interests because he partly did not realize them and partly considered them a secondary matter. However, this lack of understanding, just as the use of revelations as a propaganda tool, could not, at least in the long-term perspective, obscure the remarkable clairvoyance with which Comenius criticized the dark sides of the emerging bourgeois society and the politicians of the two most advanced countries of Europe. When he did so, he certainly did not want any return to the past, but a purposeful elimination of the already obvious or still only suspected shortcomings of modern humanity. Against a one-sided pursuit of profit he placed an appropriate distribution of material values among all needy people with funds available for the poor and the orphans, as well as for the educational, cultural and religious needs of society. Against monopolization of maritime navigation and markets he suggested as a desirable trend of economic progress guarantees for free transportation lanes and trade opportunities for all nations. He also rejected efforts to gain hegemony of power that led to wars which we are not only damaging, but, given an equitable system of nations and states, also useless. Finally, he also understood the prospects of the just emerging colonialism. „We, the Christian world, Europe, do not constitute the entire humankind, since besides us there exist hundreds of nations scattered over the face of the entire Earth", and therefore it was necessary to remember also those nations and offer them the positive values of European civilization rather than merciless exploitation.

The congress in Breda indeed resulted in a rapprochement between the two naval powers, but could not realize such a grandiose peace project. Leaving aside some of its irrational elements, Comenius' project was too far ahead of the time of its origin. It must have appeared as sheer Utopia even in the subsequent centuries. Nevertheless, his humanity-wide concept of peace, creation of safeguards in international relations through international institutions, and his efforts to bridge differences by peaceful argumentation became a great inspiration for the future. The diplomats at Breda acted as they deemed useful for their interests and quite ignored the Czech thinker. Comenius became a true „messenger of peace" for much later generations which discovered how right he was in his insight. It was only these generations which were able to understand his heroic struggle for a concept of a peaceful reform of the world. However, besides his moral example, Comenius left them yet another heritage, his General Discourse on Reform of Human Affairs, in which he explained in detail how to realize this far-reaching reform.

Universal Reform

For the Czech humanists from the Community of Brethren a „good, happy, and blessed end of life" was a supreme achievement for which a true Christian was to prepare himself throughout his journey on this Earth, and was to think of particularly in his late age. Comenius was true to this conviction and in his last years in Amsterdam often returned to the credo of his confessional ancestors. Meditation over the meaning and purpose of life and its dignified culmination gave rise to his philosophical testament **Unum necessarium** (One Necessary Thing) which he published in 1668. In it he once again reviewed his lifelong endeavours – didactic, irenic and pansophic, as well as his effort to warn humankind through published revelations – that took him through a multiple labyrinth surrounding these efforts. Although he occasionally felt his predestination for the accomplishment of great tasks, he could never shed doubts whether he had acted quite correctly. He tried to find a common denominator of his endeavours and measure it against what he thought were humanity's needs. In this final accounting he did find such a key principle which justified his efforts and offered a way out of the chaotic disharmony of the world he knew. This key principle for him was love, as reflected concretely and in the Christian spirit in the individual's relationship to other human beings and to God. What he had in mind was not a passive enjoyment of bliss, but the creative power of resurrected humanity. From this vantage point he saw the dawn of a new hope, for Comenius, the disappointed and yet optimistic old man, firmly believed that eventually humanity would emerge from all its labyrinths. He hoped that on its tortuous journey, it would also find help in his own work, in the heritage of the „tiny worm" who wanted to do much for the reform of human affairs, but so far had accomplished precious little.

His immense desire that his General Discourse of Reform of Human Affairs should illuminate the road to the future did not leave Comenius until his death. Exhausted by his advanced age and infirmity, but also by useless polemics with his opponents, Comenius returned to his principal work on his death bed, bothered by thoughts that he had not managed to prepare it for print himself. He beseeched his son Daniel to assemble the manuscripts, arrange and edit them, and attend to their comprehensive publication. Thinking of his lost homeland and of the future generations, of „the storms sweeping over Europe", Jan Amos Komenský-Comenius died in Amsterdam on November 15, 1670. A week later his body was laid to rest in the small church of the Waloon Reformed Church in nearby Naarden.

In Comenius, the Czech branch of the Community of Brethren lost its last bishop, and the Czech exiles, scattered already for half a century throughout Europe, their greatest representative. However, his work continued to live and the General Discourse continued to follow the calvary of its author. Daniel Komenský and the Czech scholar Kristián Nigrin did indeed arrange the preserved manuscripts, but these were never published. Fortunately, the manuscript did not disappear and found its way to the archives in Halle an der Saale. A vague knowledge of its existence survived and in the 18th century it was pointed out by the German philosopher Johann Gottfried von Herder, a great admirer of Comenius. However, in the 19th and the first third of the 20th centuries, the valuable manuscript could not be found. Finally, the General Discourse was discovered by the Ukrainian philosopher and philologist Dmytro Chizhevski. His fortunate find, announced to the scientific world in 1935, made it possible to complement partial editions, prepared still by Comenius (1656 – 1662) and by his later admirers, with extremely important parts. Thanks to Czech, German another Comeniologists, Comenius' greatest work had been gradually studied, investigated and interpreted, so that in 1966, the Academia Publishing House of the Czechoslovak Academy of Sciences could finally publish the complete Latin text. This „first edition" was therefore quite belated, but it appeared in an age which already understood the significance of the General Discourse. This is why interest in Comenius' key work has not ceased since then. It is being translated into different languages and is being studied by philosophers, historians, educators and other scholars in many countries in order to find inspiration for the present as well as for the future.

Academia's two-volume edition of **De rerum humanarum emendatione consultatio catholica** – the General Discourse – has made public a text which came into being with utmost difficulty. Its first version, produced at the peak of Comenius' middle age, was lost in burning Leszno in 1656. It was an irreparable loss for him. „We are advancing slowly," he wrote in January 1657, „because what had been prepared for print was destroyed by fire and the pages pulled out of the flames or found with friends are unfinished or piecemeal. Everything must thus return to the anvil of the mind, but the frailty of old age cannot accomplish as the energy of youth." Nevertheless, and in spite of detraction caused by other tasks, Comenius accomplished a great deal of work of his General Discourse. He rewrote some parts as much as twenty-times in order to be as perfect as possible in expressing his ideas in the most effective literary manner. He did not reach his desired goal, unfortunately. Many things remained unsaid and some parts do indeed reflect the fatigue of old age. On the whole, however, Comenius produced a work of extraordinary ideological and literary grandeur.

Comenius conceived his General Discourse as a monumental architectural work where everything aimed at the basic objective – enclosing past development with a vaulting of universal reform. He subordinated its individual components as well as each of the seven parts to the overall impact of the entire work which was to launch the process of reform. What he wanted was not a literary form of a Utopia, but a project which would serve as an introduction to a real discourse on reforms or to a peace congress; he thought that such discourse – or negotiations – could take place already at the ecumenical talks in Poland in the 1640s, or, possibly, two decades later, at Breda, or some time in the future.

Comenius employed all his facilities as philosopher, educator, theologian, and preacher, and projected into his work his extensive knowledge, unusually broad outlook, as well as his bitter personal experiences. He addressed the reader's reason and sentiments, referring to all authorities that could support his reform intentions. He did not want to display his originality to be admired, but, on the contrary, underlined the links with the millenial tradition ranging from the Antiquity and the Old and New Testaments through pre-reform Christianity to the great thinkers of the Renaissance, Reformation, and humanism. However, with his accent on moral precepts and calls for an active endeavour to correct human society, he tied primarily onto his immediate forerunners, on the first, Czech reformation, on the revolutionary pathos of the Hussite movements, and on the irenic heritage of the Community of Brethren. He tried to give the final shape to this heritage in the belief that his small church would disappear but its heritage would be taken up by a „Great Community" of not merely Protestans and Christians, but of all people in general, that from the upheaval of his days would emerge a human society cleansed by its suffering and newly organized under the principles of peace and justice.

In the introduction to the General Discourse, Comenius addressed intellectuals and those in power with a reminder of their tremendous responsibility for improving the existing, dismal state of affairs. He did not hide the fact that appeals for reform had been repeatedly made in the past but without any result. In his opinion, this negative experience should not lead to scepticism and passivity. Differences of view cannot remain forever an insurmountable barrier, and concern that the final objective may not be attained should not overshadow hope for at least a partial and gradual improvement. However, it is necessary to begin with the awareness that a change for the better cannot be attained by force but only by mutual conviction and by search for a common road. People should look for what binds them and leave their differences for the time being until future development may settle them. A quest for a sincere understanding of truth should convince and win over those who at first will not agree.

The actual introduction to the General Discourse is the first part of Comenius' reform work **Panegersia** (Universal Awakening), in which he proceeds from the premise that the disturbed society of the 17th century is markedly manifested in three basic fields of human activity, which do not meet their purpose. Philosophy or, in the broader sense, science do not reconciliate man with the objects surrounding him, religion does not lead to harmony of conscience with God, and politics cannot ensure peace among people. Politics in particular suffers from great defects. It should settle the contradiction between man's natural desire for freedom and voluntariness on the one hand, and the need for unity and order on the other hand. However, contemporary politicians lack the intellectual and moral qualifications for mastering the extremely exacting art of guiding society and at the same time respecting human freedom. Not understanding their tasks, rulers act arbitrarily, treating people like cattle, and instead of safeguarding peace and order, are engaged in petty power conflicts and wage unnecessary wars. Philosophy, too, has similarly failed in that instead of guiding people to true understanding and knowledge, it presents for belief distorting dogmas, while religion does not encourage people to work effectively for goodness, but leads to fanaticism and intolerance.

However – as Comenius firmly believed – resignation is not inherent in man, but rather a constant aspiration for improvement. Since all past reform efforts have failed – precisely because of their partiality – it is necessary to strive for a universal reform. The time is propitious because the dynamic development of society has created the essential conditions. Growth of manufacture, commerce and transport at the threshold of the New Age did away with the former isolation of small groups of people and regions. A new way of life produced a natural community that overcame the boundaries of individual countries and continents. „If then we are all citizens of a single world, what prevents us from . . . hoping that we shall all become a single society, well ordered and truly and properly bound by the same sciences, laws, and religion?", asks Comenius in the introduction to his General Discourse, and offers this preliminary answer: if the desire for improvement is inherent in man, on the theoretical level the road to a reform of human society is open. What is now necessary, of course, is that the learned and the powerful of this world should get together, especially those who are dissatisfied with the current state of affairs. For it is their task to seek ways of a practical reform and of attaining universal harmony.

In the quest for reform, methodological guidance was to be provided by the second volume of the General Discourse, entitled **Panaugia** (Universal Enlightenment). Proceedings from his earlier **Via lucis** (The Way of Light), Comenius showed in it how the growth of humanity's cultural level increased the intensity of the light which steadily forced out the darkness of ignorance. While our early ancestors knew only the lower classes of this school of civilization, the subsequent generations also passed through its secondary school, and the people of the present era stand at the threshold of the academy. Their task is to examine the sources of this light, which include nature, the human mind, and the Holy Script; however, in order to win for the reform process also adherents of other religions, the Jews and the Muslims in particular, it was necessary to know thoroughly not only the Old and the New Testaments but also the Koran. Comenius' ecumenism was obviously exceedings the bounds of Christianity and was aiming at humanity as a whole.

The process of tearing down the barriers deflecting the light of civilization was to be assisted by the third, fourth, and fifth volumes of the General Discourse, devoted to things, the mind, and the language. Comenius tried to explain the structure of the universe and the findings relating to it in his book **Pansophia** (Universal Wisdom); he himself called it also **Pantaxia** to indicate that his intent was not a simple description of things but an assessment of knowledge about them and their interrelationship. This large volume is one of the less comprehensive from the literary point of view, and yet it is the key to the entire work. The author selected from the immense amount of knowledge what he considered to be essential for systematic education and especially what expressed the relationship between nature and man. In doing so, he depicted man as a creator who, while remaining dependent on nature, modified it by his work and gave it a new purpose and goal. Besides technical skills he also acquired other abilities, in particular self-domination and administration of interhuman affairs and relations. Thus he built on natural foundations a world of human labour, morality, and spirit.

It was precisely in this sphere, that it was most essential to cultivate the mind, which is the topic of the next volume entitled **Pampaedia** (Universal Education). It sums up Comenius' lifelong experience and knowledge in the area of school and educational reform. However, he subordinated individual ideas and suggestions to a grander design and drew up the project of an all-encompassing system of education. He proceeded from his belief that human nature was good but had to be subjected to purposeful education. Gradual education, which was a process of gradual illumination of the human mind, was taking place both in the life of the individual and in the entire history of humankind. Truly good education could settle the conflict between every individual's desire for freedom and the need of an orderly social system, because it led the individual towards voluntarily advancing to the common goal of humanity. An essential prerequisite of success was a universal education of all people, irrespective of their property, social position, or nationality. It was precisely the availability of education to all members of a nation and to all nations, which promised for the future a uniform approach to cultural values. Education permeating man's entire life, from the preparatory, prenatal period to late age, would inject harmony into the life of every individual and would lead him towards participation in the process of building a united, reconciled and harmonious world.

Comenius considered verbal communication to be an important instrument of understanding among nations. In the 17th century he was not alone in realizing the uncontainable retreat of Latin from its earlier position of universal language of the learned. As an educator he knew quite well how difficult it was to learn this dead language and that even earlier, Latin could not become the instrument of education of all people. Therefore, in the volume entitled **Panglottia** (Universal Language) he considered the possibility of creating an artificial language, and included it in the system of reform. He wished such a language to combine the advantages of Hebrew, Greek and Latin, as well as of a number of living languages, ranging from English and German to Czech and even Turkish. The new language was to be most lucid and easily learned by logically combining things, terms, and words, and would not be burdened by any irregularities. While Comenius proposed some guiding principles for compiling an artificial language, he did not intend to realize the project himself because he felt that devising a universal language was possible only after pansophy had been completed, and, in addition, he preferred that an international group of learned people should do the work. He would have liked to see the realization of such a universally acceptable language which would facilitate quick communication, exchange of cultural values between nations, and brotherhood of all people. He wished that „all who meet anywhere could like brothers and sisters . . . greet each other and by mutually addressing each other inform each other of all that is necessary".

Comenius did suspect that difficulties might arise in the application of a uniform language once it was created, and therefore also proposed other options. The most impressive of them was his humanistic appeal to learn and develop all national languages which were not to be suppressed even by a possibly successful **panglottia** – the universal language. His objective was to achieve such an advance of every language, which would make it possible to translate into it fully all pansophic works. He did not have in mind only the nations of Europe, and constantly thought of all other non-European nations and tribes as well. He considered it a natural duty of the Europeans who so far only exploited the other continents to help spiritually enrich and cultivate the less advanced languages. However, he urged them not to act as domineering teachers but as fellow-pupils, and they were in particular to learn thoroughly the languages of the overseas nations and thereby promote mutual understanding. Whether on the basis of a universal language, or through mutual learning of other national languages, this form of communication was to improve substantially, and in the process of bringing different nations closer to each other was to help break the barriers of the boundaries between countries and continents.

In the preceding parts of his General Discourse, dealing with the penetration of the light of civilization into the dark labyrinths of things, the mind, and languages, Comenius paved the way for an outline of a universal reform of the world. In the key part of the General Discourse, entitled **Panorthosia**, meaning universal reform, he discussed a new philosophy – or education – a new religion, and new politics. He was convinced that all these spheres of man's spiritual activity had to be based on a universal concept of humanity and had to be safeguarded by worldwide institutions. The moving forces behind his project were his certainty that by nature, man was endowed with an „insatiable desire for enlightenment", and his chiliastic faith in the institution of a „new age" which had to be systematically prepared.

Comenius considered the questions of reform on the theoretical, practical, as well as applicability levels. He reached the conclusion that changes for the better could not be attained by force or by hegemony, but solely through conviction and voluntary acceptance by all. It was necessary to seek what was uniting rather than dividing individuals and nations, to realize the relative nature of truth, and to find in contradictory assertions a core acceptable to both parties in dispute. In the theological sphere this meant doing away with dogmas and building a new religion superior to the older religious systems and founded only on rational truths, the authority of the Holy Scriptures, and firm moral discipline. It was precisely such a religion, Comenius believed, that by its rational content could win a universal acceptance by Christians, Jews, Muslims, and pagans. This would give rise to a universal church whose institutional centre would be a world consistory. Similarly, the new philosophy – identical with pansophy – would also be accepted precisely because it would encompass all the wisdom acquired through the senses, by reason, or by revelation. Its institutional safeguard would be an assembly of light, in other words an international academy of education and science, which would strive for the spread of uniform education throughout the world.

Comenius remarkably elaborated his idea of new politics, of a reformed administration of public affairs. Its main task would be the institution and maintenance of lasting justice, order, and peace. This would be the objective for which institutions at all levels would collaborate, and on the worldwide scale it would be pursued by an international peace court, or world senate, which would be furnished with great jurisdiction. It would attend not only to the maintenance of peace among states, but also to the maintenance of order and justice in individual states, because the two are inseparably linked. Therefore, too, the world senate would supervise national and local courts of justice and laws, so that their decisions and provisions would not run counter to the superior, universally human principles and universal law which would derive only from natural law and the laws of God. Interhuman relations would be corrected through a reform of all the components of public administration, involving a definition of their rights and duties relating to the social order and publicly beneficial work. The same objective would be followed by a reform of the family, every member of which should live in the future in a disciplined, modest and diligent manner in the spirit of the tradition of the Community of Brethren and in harmony with Calvinist ideals. From this ensued the duty of every adult person to work for personal, family, and community interests, but also the duty of public administration to provide everybody with the opportunity to obtain an appropriate employment. Therefore, people should not be classed according to the feudal estates but according to the role they played in society by their work. Since „the people's welfare should be the supreme law of any republic and any kingdom"; officials should be subject to public control in order to prevent abuse of their authority; if necessary, they would be deposed. Similarly, brutal and immoral people occupying leading posts should be removed, just as sycophants and informers who are „the most malignant kind of people".

Comenius' project goes into considerable detail in many respects, including ideas about the way people would eat and dress in the new society. However, this penchant for detail, typical of the times, does not basically disturb the general character of his work. All the concrete details were actually meant as proposals to be dealt with by a world council that was to meet in the foreseeable future at Venice, a place that was easily accessible to representatives of not only European but also Asian and African nations. The council was to bring together statesmen, theologians and scholars, who would discuss the suggestions contained in the General Discourse; in the spirit of a free consent of all the participants, the council was to agree on the means of instituting and preserving unity and peace. The measures they adopted were then to be implemented not only by the three main world institutions (the international court of peace, the world academy, and the world consistory), but also by bodies furnished with executive powers, democratically elected from all nations, and active on regional, continental, and worldwide levels. A world coordinating assembly was to meet every ten years, which would hold its sessions successively in Europe, Asia, Africa, and America, so that the equality of all the continents would not be disturbed even in this respect.

However, a world of peace and prosperity could be created only by a common effort of all nations and especially of their representatives. Therefore, it was they – statesmen, scholars, and theologians – who bore immense responsibility towards all humanity. Comenius urgently recalled this responsibility in the final part of the General Discourse, entitled **Pannuthesia** (Universal Encouragement). He stressed that at the time when the great majority of mankind was living in spiritual poverty and material want, subsidiary interests and petty quarrels had to swept away in order to permit the solution of the most important problems. After all, there was no greater and nobler task for all learned people than to seek ways of a thorough reform of human affairs!

Comenius' grandiose vision of a happy future of the human race proceeded mostly from speculative considerations and was encouraged by his chiliastic belief in an early coming of the kingdom of Christ on Earth. Nevertheless, Comenius was able to overcome this determinant ensuing from the period in which he lived, and to look beyond the bounds of the expiring feudal and the emerging capitalist social orders. Proceeding from the European cultural tradition and with a rare openmindedness to all human values, he created a hopeful image of progressive historical development. After a life filled with disillusionment, he offered to mankind an optimistic prospect of advancement towards peace and unity through a democratic system of interhuman relations and equality of nations. This prospect, which by far transcended Comenius' own times, has lost nothing of its attraction even at the threshold of the third millenium.

Comenius' Work in the Changes of Time

No great work is unequivocally accepted by its contemporaries. The less so could this be expected in the case of a thinker who wanted to change the world so radically. In his universalism Comenius touched on so many contradictory and particular interests, and frequently offered such unusual formulas for solving the problems of his time, that besides approval he also ran into strong opposition. While his simpler and materially indisputable proposals, especially in the area of language instruction, were mostly accepted with approval, this was certainly not true of his more complex projects – frequently not only because of their revolutionary character, but also because Comenius ran counter to the then prevalent and sometimes even more progressive currents of thought. Already some of his proposals for a general school reform were ignored, and the more so did this disinterest or resistance apply to his project of a universal reform of society, which – it should be remembered – was known to his contemporaries only in its small part.

Comenius found a few advocates who especially in England promoted his pansophic ideas, and he also had some adherents in Germany and other European countries. However, in the latter half of the 17th century, his opponents became increasingly vociferous simultaneously from two sides. While the rationalists from the ranks of the Socinians and Cartesians viewed Comenius as a dreamer, the church dogmatists saw him as an irresponsible rationalist who placed in doubt and even denied untouchable theological dogmas. The resulting sharp polemics indicated that Comenius' international authority had greatly waned towards the end of his life, and many people may have believed that the name of this Czech exile would soon fall into oblivion. This was wrong, of course, because Comenius' work radiated too strong ideas to be completely ignored and forgotten by the subsequent generations.

Comenius' heritage was closer to that current of European thinking, which would not accept a one-sided scientific and analytical approach to reality, but tried to view the world as an entity and especially to study man's position therein. In this universalistic current of thinking, the man closest to Comenius was the great German philosopher of the Baroque period, Cottfried Wilhelm Leibnitz (1646 – 1716), who frequently referred to Comenius' ideas and proposals, and in many respects arrived at a similar, though already more thoroughly worked-out solution of humanity's universal problems. In the history of European philosophy Leibnitz unwittingly overshadowed Comenius' pansophy, but he paid his debt to his indirect teacher in a Latin poem of homage. Shortly after Comenius' death, in 1671, Leibnitz offered this prophecy in his poem:

„The time will come, Comenius, when hosts of nobleminded men will honour what Thou hast done alone, honouring as well the dreat of Thy hopes."

The road leading to full appreciation of Comenius' efforts for universal reform was, of course, a long and complex one. After Leibnitz, his heritage was also taken up at the turn of the 17th and 18th centuries by German pietists who underlined in particular the religious aspects of Comenius' work. The pietists held that the religiousness of the orthodox Protestant churches was formalistic and unsatisfying, and countered it with the ideal of improvement of life in all spheres of human activity. They found great inspiration in Comenius' project of universal reform and on the theological level especially his work **Unum necessarium.** In the spirit of Comenius' views, it was especially the Pietists led by August Hermann Francke (1663 – 1727), a theologian and educator in Halle an der Saale, who evolved their ideology focussed on reform of the family, education, and society. This Comenian renaissance at the beginning of the 18th century not only revived for some time the reform ideas of the Czech thinker, but also helped to preserve his writings on universal reform. It is to this short renaissance that we must thank for bridging the long period of time when Comenius' work was almost forgotten.

The mainstream of European thinking in the 18th century followed quite a different channel. The emerging era of enlightenment accentuated an analytical and critical approach to reality and had not much understanding for earlier attempts at an all-emcompassing synthesis. The Frenchman Pierre Bayle (1647 – 1706), a representative of early enlightenment, devoted considerable attention to Comenius in his **Dictionnaire historique et critique.** This encyclopaedia was first published in the period 1695 – 1697, and by 1740 had been re-issued in five French editions and in German translation. It gained immense popularity among the adherents of Enlightenment and for most of them it was the only source of information about Comenius. This was significant because in his rationalistic criticism, Bayle heaped upon Comenius the most scathing condemnation ever written about him. He did praise Comenius as an important grammarian who had secured his immortality with his textbook **Ianua linguarum reserata**, but rejected his broader educational objectives. Bayle utterly denounced Comenius' pansophic works and in particular his opinion of revelations. Bayle wrote that Comenius was „insanely captivated by prophecies and similar cases of dangerous fanaticism", and accused him of being a fraud and blatant profiteer. Bayle, one of the founders of modern historical criticism' uncritically accepted the subjective denunciation of Comenius by his contemporary opponents and also embraced personal insults which were later shown to have been completely unfounded. He made all this sound plausible by his seemingly uninvolved objectivity. In fact, however, he projected into his criticism of revelations the current ideological struggle within the French Huguenot movement, in which he was personally involved. In his literary portrait of Comenius he mostly dealt with his own problems and in the person of Comenius he scathingly denounced his own opponents from the end of the 17th century, who by chance also believed in prophecies.

These circumstances, only recently explained by the Czech historian Josef Válka, were naturally unknown to the Enlightened. For otherwise they might have forgotten Comenius as a personality who did deserve respect but who already belonged to the past and had nothing to tell them. However, thanks to Bayle, they took a completely negative scientific and moral approach to Comenius, which survived the entire 18th century. Only a few of the enlightened philosophers were able to shed this stereotype. One of them was the German writer Johann Gottfried von Herder (1744 – 1803) who in his thinking already presaged the Romantic effort to create a new, poetic synthesis of the world. It was Herder who positively appreciated Comenius' idea of the human being as the creator of human history, actively striving to improve himself. Such praiseworthy but only isolated returns to Comenius could not, of course, bring about his rehabilitation. The road to understanding and duly appreciating Comenius' work had to be sought first and foremost by his fellow-countrymen.

Comenius had not been forgotten in his homeland either when he was in exile or after his death. Naturally, as representative of the persecuted

Community of Brethren and as a political opponent of the ruling Hapsburgs, he ranked among the officially undesirable figures of the national past. And yet, his remarkable contribution to improved language instruction had to be recognized even by the Jesuits who fully dominated Czech education after the battle on White Mountain; in 1667 they published Comenius' **Ianua linguarum reserata** in a Latin-Czech-German version as a textbook for their students. The prominent Czech Baroque historian Bohuslav Balbín (1621 – 1688), who was an unorthodox Jesuit, also appreciated Comenius' greatness as an educator and respected his rare religious tolerance. Comenius' name remained known to Czech historians throughout the 18th century, but his true rediscovery did not occur until the beginning of the 19th century.

The merit for changing the opinion on Comenius and for his re integration in the history of Czech culture belongs to František Palacký (1798 – 1876), the founder of modern Czech historiography and author of the political programme of the revived Czech nation. In 1829, Palacký published the first comprehensive biography of Comenius. He succeeded in overcoming the older, narrow view of Comenius as a mere didact. First of all, he praised the exceptional significance of the Czech-written works of Comenius, so much so that he gave him the stature of the so far greatest Czech writer. However, Palacký did not merely praise Comenius' contribution to his own nation, but tried to rid his heritage of the sediment of the one-sided criticism from the Enlightenment period. He tried to explain Comenius' controversial belief in revelations by historical and psychological reasons, but accentuated most strongly his contribution to the reform of school education. He gave Comenius the merit for launching the process of change in European education from the dominant theology and Latin philology to realistic subjects and pursuit of national language instruction and study. Thereby, according to Palacký, Comenius „paved the way for the industrial and naturalist spirit of modern Europe", became a spokesman for the interests of the emerging bourgeoisie, and thus joined the ranks of „the most remarkable men of all ages and all nations".

Soon thereafter, the interest in Comenius was raised to a higher level by the great Czech natural scientist Jan Evangelista Purkyně (1787 – 1869). At the time when he was professor of physiology at the University of Wroclaw, Purkyně devoted much attention to producing a bibliography of sources on Czech history in foreign archives and libraries. He visited Leszno in 1836 and then on several more occasions, and in the archive

of the local chapter of the Evangelical Reformed Church he discovered
a number of until then unknown Comenius' manuscripts. He was instrumental in arranging for the purchase of most of these manuscripts by the
Museum of the Czech Kingdom (today the National Museum) in Prague,
where they were soon made accessible to researchers. Since the middle
of the 19th century, the previously unknown manuscripts (the Czech Didactics, correspondence, and others) were gradually published and greatly
changed the scholarly and the public approach to Comenius. While earlier
he had been considered almost exclusively a linguistic didact and a personality of Czech literature, he was now being increasingly gaining prominence as an outstanding pedagogue with a broad educational concept. This
is how his heritage was taken up mainly by Czech and Moravian teachers.
It was they who made Comenius gain stature as one of the greatest and
best known personalities of Czech history, and he became a symbol
of resistance to national oppression in the Austro-Hungarian monarchy.

It was this national liberation spirit that permeated the first nationwide
celebrations honouring Comenius, held in 1871 (since the proper date
of Comenius' death was not known, the commemoration of the bicentenial
of his death took place belatedly) and especially in 1892. Against the
opposition of the Austrian authorities and a part of the Roman Catholic
hierarchy, practically the entire Czech nation manifested its allegiance
to „the educator of his nation and the teacher of all nations". However,
what was of greater importance was the fact that the celebrations with
their speeches did not remain an isolated event, but that the broad public
interest evoked by them sparked the growth of very intensive research
on Comenius and his work, which eventually crystallized into a separate
field of study – Comeniology. The first attempts then followed to proceed
from the publication of individual writings to a complete edition of Comenius' works. Due to the exceptional range of Comenius' literary production
and to the difficulty of its critical edition, this was an extremely demanding
task which has not been fully realized to this day.

At the end of the 19th century, the interest in Comenius spread beyond
the Czech environment. An outstanding personality among the Comeniologists of those days was the Slovak scholar Ján Kvačala (1862 – 1934),
professor at the University of Tartu, who raised the study of Comenius'
educational system to a higher level within the broader framework
of history of philosophy; Kvačala also greatly contributed to coordination
of Comeniological studies as editor of the journal **Archiv pro bádání**

o životě a spisech J. A. Komenského (Archive of Studies on the Life and Writings of J. A. Comenius), launched in 1910 and published to this day under the name **Acta Comeniana.**

No less important was the emergence of an organizational base for Comeniological studies abroad. An attempt was made in Russia to publish a selection of Comenius' works, but an especially important centre of these studies came into existence in Germany. It was the **Comenius-Gesellshaft** founded in Berlin in 1890 within the framework of preparations for celebrations marking the 300th anniversary of Comenius' birth. The interest this Comenian Society attracted is indicated by the fact that already in 1896 it associated 1,200 individual and collective members from sixteen countries. They included educators, theologians, politologists, as well as public personalities, all of whom pursued the objective of presenting Comenius' work to the public and of preserving his heritage for the future generations. Thanks to Ján Kvačala and other prominent members, the Society discovered new, important sources which were published between 1892 and 1934 in the journal **Monathefte der Comenius Gesellschaft.** However, in addition to promoting knowledge about Comenius, the Society also strove for improvement of the existing school system and educational methods in the spirit of Comenius' principles. It deserves credit for having given the interest in Comenius' work a comprehensive character and considerable international scope.

This promotion of Comenius' ideas abroad was parallelled by a growth of Czech Comeniology which obtained support after 1918 from the newly founded Czechoslovak Republic. The official policy and the first Czechoslovak President, Tomáš Garrigue Masaryk, personally, took up Comenius' heritage, just as the non-Catholic church circles. This was especially true of the Evangelical Church of Czech Brethren, which at the end of 1918 adopted as its ideological base – besides the 1575 Czech Confession – the Confession of the Community of Brethren, which Comenius adapted and published in Amsterdam in 1662. Although Protestant historians and theologians became deeply involved in Comeniological studies, Comeniology did not become a pronouncedly confessional field of study. On the contrary, ever new discoveries of Comenius' key works, made by Czechoslovak and foreign scholars at Halle, in Leningrad, Sheffield, and elsewhere, opened new, unforeseen prospects. The experts and later also the general public gradually abandoned the earlier, simplified view of Comenius as a „teacher of nations", and increasingly understood him as a complex, dynamically developing personality of an exceptional scope of knowledge and vision, ranging from education, philosophy and theology to politics and efforts to bring about a universal reform of society.

In the period between the two World Wars, a question of scholarly interest as much as of piety was finally settled, namely the long-lasting doubt about the last resting place of Comenius whose grave was finally identified by historical and archaeological research in the Dutch town of Naarden. For the once Waloon church had been closed in 1819 and was turned into military barracks in 1861. In spite of problems caused by the removal and loss of tombstones from the church whose interior was also reconstructed in the 19th century, experts succeeded in finding and identifying Comenius' grave in 1929. A few years later, in 1933, the Dutch government decided to turn over the property rights to the entire former church to Czechoslovakia. This generous move created the optimum conditions for the establishment of a dignified Comenius Memorial. Thanks to sculptor Jaroslav Horejc, painter Jaroslav Benda, and other Czech artists, a modern but most impressive mausoleum came into being, whose interior decoration recalls the principal stations in the life of the eternal pilgrim, as well as his major works. Opened in 1937, the memorial is visited annually by thousands of people from different parts of the world, who come there to pay their respect to the great man.

The Second World War overshadowed for several years the ideas championed by the „messenger of peace", but the experience of that conflagration's unprecedented horrors created a social environment in which Comenius' work has acquired a new significance. The world began to understand with greater clarity his irenism and his ceaseless search for ways leading to international rapport. Comenius' heritage was taken up by the United Nations Organization which in a modern form embodies Comenius' idea of an international peace organization and which therefore adopted him as one of its „patrons". At its general conference in Delhi in 1956, the United Nations Educational, Scientific and Cultural Organization, too, embraced the ideas of Comenius as „one of the first proponents of ideas that have inspired UNESCO since its very founding". A year later, the World Peace Council described Comenius as a classic of „ideas of peace and human brotherhood, which have enriched the cultural heritage of all mankind".

Comenius' native country as well took a new approach to his heritage. It was expressed by the first minister of education in the liberated Czechoslovak Republic, and later the first president of the Czechoslovak Academy of Sciences, Zdeněk Nejedlý (1878 – 1962), in an article publi-shed in 1947. Nejedlý underlined that Comenius' identification with the feudal order and his closeness to religion posed to obstacles to reception of his ideas by the people's democratic and socialist systems. On the contrary, Comenius was still an unchallenged model because his „humanis-tic and people's school continued to be an ideal which ... can be better and more profoundly approached under the new social order". However, Comenius' heritage was also a source of historical optimism springing forth from the Hussite revolution and expressed in the works of the greatest thinkers of the Czech past, „from John Hus through Comenius to Palacký and Masaryk". Nejedlý viewed Comenius' work as a major contribution to humanity by the Czech nation, and in this sense, too, he formulated the duty of Czech scholars to make accessible Comenius' entire work on a priority basis.

A fine opportunity for institutionalizing this programme were the cele-brations marking the 300th anniversary of the first publication of the **Opera didactica omnia** and of the **Orbis sensualium pictus** observed in the years 1956 – 1958. In March 1956 the Czechoslovak government adopted a reso-lution calling for the publication of a critical edition of all of Come-nius' works (it is being published since 1969 under the title **J. A. Comenii Opera omnia**) as well as of an extensive selection of his works for the broader public. This decision led to the formation of several institutions concerned with the study and publication of Comenius' heritage.

These institutions include, in the first place, the J. A. Comenius Paeda-gogical Institute within the framework of the Czechoslovak Academy of Sciences, which has a special division of Comeniology and history of the school and of paedagogy; it is this institute which bears the main burden of the exacting task of publishing Comenius' works and of their scientific interpretation. The main centre of documentation of Comenius' life and work and of the latter's impact was established in 1957 in the Comenius Museum in Uherský Brod. The network of professional Comeniological institutions is complemented by the J. A. Comenius Paedagogical Museum in Prague and the J. A. Comenius District Museum in Přerov. The earlier mentioned two institutions publish specialized periodicals – the interna-tional journal **Acta Comeniana** (in Prague) and **Studia Comeniana et histo-rica**, a scientific journal for Comeniology, 16th to 18th century history, and for information about Comenius' native region, which is being published in Uherský Brod. Both periodicals carry articles and reports by Czechoslovak and foreign scholars, and reports on Comeniological research which has been rapidly growing in recent decades in many countries of Europe but also in Asia and America.

A highly reputed partner of the Czechoslovak institutions abroad is the **Comeniusforschungsstelle** in the Paedagogical Institute of Ruhr University at Bochum in the Federal Republic of Germany. Headed by one of the world's foremost Comeniologists, Klaus Schaller, this research centre, established in 1970, is engaged in extensive publication and scientific organization activities. It is publishing the journal **Mitteilungsblatt**, containing studies, reports on developments in the field of Comeniology, and bibliographies, as well as a **Schriften** series, containing important monographs, source materials, and reports on Comeniological conferences.

Thanks to the dedicated effort of many Comeniologists, the name Comenius has become known to people throughout the world, and the gradual publication of his works – not only in Latin and his mother tongue Czech, but also in all the world's major as well as other languages – Comenius' heritage is becoming the spiritual property of people in all the continents. Great credit is due for their dozens of books and hundreds of articles and studies about Comenius, and for difficult translations of his writings into their national languages to scholars especially in Britain, Bulgaria, China, Denmark, France, the Federal Republic of Germany, Hungary, Italy, Japan, the Netherlands, Norway, Poland, Rumania, the Soviet Union, the United States, and to a lesser degree in other countries; nor must we forget the deserving publishing activity of the United Nations Educational, Scientific and Cultural Organization, UNESCO.

Although the knowledge of Comenius' work in all its aspects is not quite satisfactory and differs from one country to another, there is no longer the danger that this thinker will be forgotten. In fact, Comeniologists must cope with the opposite problem, namely that, just as in other dynamically expanding fields of research, the volume of new information in Comeniology is growing so fast, that it is becoming increasingly difficult to digest it all. Here, an important role is being played by scientific conferences held in many countries, most frequently, of course, in Czechoslovakia. Regular international Comeniological colloquiums – **Colloquium Comenianum Hunnobrodense** – are held every year in Uherský Brod, in the area were Comenius was born – and are instrumental especially in clarifying still unsettled questions, such as, for example, the until recently disputed

problems of Comenius' views on natural science, his approach to revelations, or his concept of human activity. Coordination of international
research was greatly promoted by large symposiums held several times
between 1957 and 1986, which brought together scholars from practically
the entire world to exchange views on Comenius' contribution to the
development of education, science and culture, and to efforts to safeguard
peace and to reform human society.

Modern Comeniology has cleared up many problems, and the image
of Comenius has acquired in general quite distinct features. It is now
beyond any doubt that the heritage of this 17th century Czech thinker has
lost nothing of its significance even four centuries after his birth. In spite
of the occasional doubts of its creator and its rejection by subsequent
generations, and even in spite of all the marks left on it by the times of its
origin, Comenius' work is today rightly gaining in significance. Obviously,
too, this work is still waiting for its consistent reintegration into the history
of world culture and for an assessment of its importance for the future.

Heritage for the Future

An all-round evaluation of Comenius' work will be the task of a large international conference – The Heritage of J. A. Comenius and Man's Education for the 21st Century – which will be held in Prague on the occasion of the 400th anniversary of Comenius' birth and which will bring together prominent scientists, educators, political and religious personalities, and representatives of culture and mass media from all parts of the world. This conference, scheduled for March 1992, will thus offer the opportunity to draw up a balance sheet of past work and outline prospects for the future. This is not the place to presage the results of the meeting which will be able to proceed not only symbolically from the General Discourse on Reform of Human Affairs. Let us therefore try to sum up only very briefly, in a few final sentences, what has been said here so far.

Comenius' work came into being under extremely dramatic circumstances in a period fraught with conflicts, which we generally describe as the beginning of the transition of European society from feudalism to capitalism. It was a period of protracted economic crisis, of the bourgeois revolution in England, and of ceaseless wars which swept through the entire continent. Parallelling the accumulating conflicts in the economic, social, military, political, and ideological spheres was a process of profound differentiation of Europe. On one side was the retarded, feudal part, which after 1620 also included Comenius' homeland, and on the other side the rapidly advancing countries of early capitalism, which Comenius came to know as an exile. However, it was also a period of revolutionary change in science and in the dominant view of the world. In the first half of the 17th century, Comenius came to know the advanced West European milieu, embraced as a model of the social order bourgeois rule, and considered as the best form of government a monarchy under control of the estates and later, towards the end of his life, a republic of the type existing in the Low Countries. However, he never abandoned his efforts to help his native country which was taking quite a different course. Nor did he ever accept the negative aspects of the capitalist way of life, in particular the quest for profit and the merciless exploitation of overseas colonies. Proceedings from the tradition of European thought, he sought alternative ways of development which would help bridge differences and conflicts between individuals and nations. In his concrete proposals he was inspired by the tragic experience of the Community of Brethren and considered the possibility of creating a „Great Union" of all humanity.

This search could not avoid an occasional groping for the proper course to follow in a labyrinth which symbolized to Comenius the world in which he lived. He was not always able to find the right bearings in the ever-changing situation, and given his very limited influence with the rulers of the European states, his political activity remained mostly futile. The means he used to influence public opinion, in particular his publication of revelations, were fully subservient to the pre-critical stage in the history of social philosophy. Later generations rightly rejected these aspects of his work, just as they rejected his efforts to save the geocentric concept of the universe or to build a perpetuum mobile. However, over the span of time they also recognized that these errors and weak points were certainly not the mainstays of his work.

Comenius remained throughout his life a profoundly religious individual and representative of a small and yet ethically and culturally ambitious Evangelical church, the Community of Brethren. It should not be, therefore, surprising that he thought in religious terms and that he found strong inspiration – proceedings from European heresies and the revolutionary Hussite movement – in the chiliastic belief in the coming of Christ's millenial kingdom on Earth. Nevertheless, Comenius would not accept religious dogma and, whenever he could, he strove for understanding between members of different churches as well as for a practical application of religious tolerance. An all-round analysis of Comenius' work from the viewpoints of Protestants and Catholics, believers and atheists, Marxists, existentialists, and proponents of other philosophical trends has clearly shown one important fact, namely that Comenius was able to rise above confessional aspects to the point where his ideological heritage can be accepted as a serious inspiration by adherents of different philosophical and ideological trends, for they have reached the identical conclusion that its substance – in particular his reform and irenical ideas are universally valid.

Comenius' philosophical views were being shaped in close identity with ancient Greek and Roman, mediaeval, and Renaissance traditions, and at the same time in opposition to the emerging physical and mechanistic concept of the world. Although some of Comenius' ideas may have appeared „outdated" from the vantage point of the 17th and 18th centuries, from the long-term perspective they were of exceptional significance. They preindicated a dynamic and dialectical understanding of natural reality and laid stress on an organic link between individual phenomena, on the inner quality of things, and on historical development. For Comenius, it was practical activity, creative human work, rather than passive contemplation, which were the decisive factor in the process of reforming human life, society, and the world. Man, furnished with will and free by nature, became the key subject of history. It was this elevation of man to the stature of a free creator with the prospect of self-realization in the course of history, which constitutes Comenius' priceless contribution to world thinking. It presaged the development towards German classical philosophy at the turn of the 18th and 19th centuries, and towards socialist ideas. Comenius thereby pointed to a more humane alternative to Cartesianism as a way to the modern world.

Universal education became the means of reshaping the world towards harmony and elevation of man to humanism. It was not to be limited merely to schooling for a future profession, but was to permeate the individual's entire life. Guide him towards true freedom and conscious humanity. Comenius viewed the individual's education as development of his natural abilities, as creation of a balance between personal freedom and social order, as a process of nurturing of the consciousness that every individual is responsible for the entire community and that the community is responsible for its every individual member. This concept of education gave rise to Comenius' proposals for the evolvement of universal culture and integration of scientific disciplines, for a consistent utilization of all spiritual values for the public good, and for a close link between theory and practice. People, improved by lifelong education were to realize universal reform and enjoy its fruits – harmony between man and nature, rational welfare, tolerance among individuals, and peace among nations.

Naturally, the forms of social organization change according to the attained level of humanity's material and spiritual development, as well as on the given social order. The differences between the 17th and 20th centuries are vast. Therefore, even Comenius' concrete proposals of a system of interhuman and international relations cannot be viewed as a formula for solving contemporary problems. What can be done is to approach Comenius' entire project as a challenge – to assess how these problems came into being and how ways of solving them appeared already centuries ago. For Comenius is close to us not only with his desire to reform human affairs, but also because of his idea of a harmonious, free, and socially responsible man as the realizer of such reform. It is in today's uneasy and divided world, where his words from the General Discourse about the need of bringing people close together for a happy future, no matter how distant they may be today from each other socially, ideologically, ethnically, or in their form of government, sound especially urgent: „We are all on the same ship in Europe, observing how the other continents, on their ships, are tumbling on the ocean of human woes . . ."

The deep contradictions in the development of modern civilization have crystallized into a most dangerous shape. Finding their global solution will be the task of the generations that will enter the 21st century. It is to them that Comenius has offered over the span of centuries a most generous gift – the consciousness of man's freedom and of his responsibility for the harmonious advancement of the human race – and by his own life has given an example that inspires creative deeds.

List of main biographical dates

1592 (March 28) – Jan Amos Komenský – Comenius – is born at Uherský Brod or its close vicinity
1604 – Comenius' parents die; he is being raised at Strážnice
1605 – (May 4) – Strážnice burned down by Hungarian troops
1608 – 1611 – study at the Latin school in Přerov, Moravia
1611 – 1613 – study at the Nassau Academy in Herborn
1613 (spring) – first journey to the Netherlands
1613 – 1614 – theological studies at Heidelberg
1614 – 1618 – teacher at Přerov; historical and encyclopaedical works
1616 (April) – ordained as priest of the Community of Brethren
1618 – 1621 – administrator of the Community congregation and school at Fulnek
1618 (June 19) – first marriage (with Magdalena Vizovská)
1619 – publication of Comenius' socio-critical work Letters to the Heavens
1620 – Comenius openly sympathizes with the estates' uprising against the Hapsburgs in Moravia; probably took part in welcoming the elected king Friedrich of the Palatinate
1621 (spring) – after the crushing defeat of the rebellious estates on White Mountain (November 8, 1620), the imperial troops occupy Fulnek; Comenius leaves Fulnek (winter 1621 – 1622)
1622 (spring) – Comenius' wife and both sons die
1622 – 1628 – hiding in Eastern Bohemia on the estates of Karel the Elder of Žerotín and other Protestant nobles
1622 – 1624 – working on consolation writing
1623 (May 1) – Comenius' books publicly burned in Fulnek
1623 (December) – Comenius' most important Czech work, The Labyrinth of the World, completed
1624 (September 3) – second marriage (with Dorota Cyrillová, daughter of bishop Jan Cyrill of the Community of Brethren)
1625 – 1626 – first mission abroad in the service of the Community of Brethren (Poland, Brandenburg, Moravia, the Netherlands)
1626 (summer) – meeting with the escaped Czech king Friedrich; Comenius presents to him a message from Ladislav Velen of Žerotín, the leader of the Mora-

vian exiles, and a prophecy about a positive turn of the situation in Europe and the course of the Thirty Years' War

1627 – Comenius' Map of Moravia published in Amsterdam

1628 (February 4) – departure into exile

1628 – 1641 – first stay in the Polish town of Leszno; intensively writing paedagogic and pansophic works

1628 – appointed teacher at the Leszno gymnasium and member of the leadership of the Community of Brethren

1630 – 1632 – Comenius completes Czech Didactics and other paedagogic, political, and socio-critical writings

1631 – he completes his Latin textbook **Ianua linguarum reserata** (The Open Gate of Languages) which wins him reputation throughout Europe

1632 (October) – appointed bishop and executive secretary of the Community of Brethren

1637 – 1639 – Comenius' friend Samuel Hartlib publishes his works **Conatum Comenianorum praeludia** (Preludes to Comenius' Endeavours, Oxford 1637) and **Prodromus pansophiae** (Predecessor of universal Knowledge, London 1639)

1638 – 1639 – attempts to dramatize the subject matter of instruction: the plays **Diogenes Cynicus redivivus** (Diogenes of Kynos Revived 1638) and **Abrahamus patriarcha** (1639)

1641 – 1642 – sojourn in London at the invitation of his English patrons – the Comenian Group – in particular Samuel Hartlib and John Dury; meets the Czech graphic artist Václav Hollar; writes **Via lucis** (The Way of Light), outlining the reform of society through better education

1642 (spring) – civil war prevents Comenius' work in England, turns down invitation from Cardinal Richelieu to come to France; accepts invitation from Dutch-Swedish merchant Louis de Geer to come to Sweden

1642 (June – October) – journey through the Netherlands, Northern Germany and Sweden to Swedish-dominated Elblag (Northern Poland); in September meets Swedish queen Kristina and her Chancellor Axel Oxenstierna

1642 – 1648 – stay in Elblag; works on the project of a new system of school textbooks

1644 – probably begins his greatest work, **De rerum humanarum emendatione consultatio catholica** (General Discourse on Reform of Human Affairs)

1646 – completes the textbook **Methodus linguarum novissima** (The Latest Language Instruction Method)

1646 (September – October) – journey to Sweden for new talks with Queen Kristina and Chancellor Oxenstierna

1647 (summer) – journey to Germany in attempt to assert the demands of the Czech exiles in the Peace of Westphalia

1647 – publication of **Historia persecutionum ecclesiae Bohemicae** (History of the Persecution of the Bohemian Church)

1648 (August) – return to Leszno where his second wife dies on August 26; then elected leading bishop of the scattered Community of Brethren

1648 – 1650 – second stay in Leszno

1649 (May 17) – third marriage (with Jana Gajusová)

1650 – publication in Leszno of Testament of the Dying Mother, the Community of Brethren, Comenius' moral heritage for the Czech nation

1650 – 1654 – stay in Sárospatak in the service of the Rákoczi princely family, the dynastic rulers of Transylvania; charged with reforming the princely Latin school; hopes for involvement of the Rákoczis in the struggle against the Hapsburgs

1654 – **Ianua linguarum reserata** dramatized into **Schola ludus** (School Through Play); **Gentis felicitas** (The Happiness of the Nation), addressed to György II Rákoczi, was Comenius' appeal for internal reforms in Transylvania and for joining the fight against the Hapsburgs

1654 – 1656 – third stay in Leszno

1654 – hope for English assistance and for a drive of an army of Czech exiles to liberate their country

1655 – publication of **Panegyricus Carolo Gustavo** (In Praise of Karl Gustav), urging the Swedish king to institute religious freedom in Poland

1656 (April) – Polish army burns Leszno; Comenius escapes, losing his property, library and unpublished manuscripts

1656 – 1670 – stay in Amsterdam

1657 – **Lux in tenebris** (Light in the Darkness), a complete edition of older prophecies urging continued fight against the Hapsburgs and the papacy

1657 – 1658 – publication of a four-volume collection of Comenius' paedagogical works **Opera didactica omnia** (Assembled Didactical Works), which also included the **Didactica magna** (The Great Didactics)

1658 – publication of the pictorial textbook of languages **Orbis sensualium pictus** (The World in Pictures)

1659 – 1661 – theological polemics against Dutch Socinians

1661 – **Epistola ad Montanum**, a long letter addressed to the Amsterdam printer Peter Montanus and reviewing Comenius' literary activity so far

1662 – publication of **Panegersia** (Universal Awakening) and **Panaugia** (Universal Enlightenment), the first two volumes of Comenius' lifetime work **De rerum humanarum emendatione consultatio catholica** (General Discourse on Reform of Human Affairs)

1663 – publication of **Letzte Posaun über Deutschland**, an attempt to influence the German public in favour of reform

1665 – **Lux e tenebris** (Light from the Darkness), an enlarged edition of prophecies with an appeal for reform of the world

1665 – 1670 – manuscript form of collection of notes on hopes for a reform of humanity, **Clamores Eliae** (The Pleadings of Elijah)

1667 (May) – publication in Amsterdam of **Angelus pacis** (The Messenger of Peace), calling for reconciliation between the Netherlands and England and for elimination of all wars; Comenius personally attends the Anglo-Dutch peace talks at Breda (peace concluded on July 31, 1667)

1668 – publication of philosophical testament **Unum necessarium**, appealing for peace and a harmonious life

1669 – Comenius writes an outline of his autobiographical **Continuatio admonitionis fraternae** (Continuation of fraternal admonitions)

1670 (November 15) – Comenius dies in Amsterdam

1670 (November 22) – Comenius burried in the church of the Waloon Reformed Church in Naarden

Selected Comeniological bibliography

(This bibliography lists only the most important books published about Comenius and his work in some of the world's major languages; the other listed publications are mostly furnished with summaries in one or more of these languages.)

ALT, Robert: *Der fortschrittliche Charakter der Pädagogik Komenský' s* Berlin 1954.

BEČKOVÁ, Marta: *Jan Amos Komenský a Polsko (J. A. Komenský and Poland).* Prague 1983.

BELLERATE, Bruno (ed.): *Comenio sconosciuto.* Cosenza 1984.

BIEŃKOWSKI, Tadeusz: *Komeński w nauce i tradycji.* Wrocław 1980.

BLEKASTAD, Milada: *Comenius. Versuch eines Umrisses von Leben, Werk und Schicksal des Jan Amos Komenský.* Oslo-Prague 1969.

BRITSCHGI, Gertrud: *Naturbegriff und Menschenbild bei Comenius.* Zurich 1964.

CAMMAROTA, Pasquale: *Introduzione a J. A. Comenius.* Naples 1972.

CAMMAROTA, Pasquale: *Introduzione allo studio di J. A. Comenius.* Salerno 1968.

CARAVOLAS, Jean: *Le Gutenberg de la didacographie ou Coménius et l'enseignement des langues.* Montreal 1984.

Comenio o della pedagogia. Rome 1974.

Comenius. Erkennen – Glauben – Handeln. Internationales Comenius-Colloquium Herborn 1984. Sankt Augustin 1985.

Comenius. A Symposium held ... at New York University ... to commemorate the 300th anniversary of the death of Jan Amos Comenius (Komenský). New York 1972.

Comenius and Contemporary Education. Hamburg 1970.

Comenius and Hungary. Budapest 1973.

Coménius et l'education contemporaine. Hamburg 1972.

Jan Amos Comenius. Geschichte und Aktualität 1670 – 1970. Vols. I-II, Glashütten im Taunus 1971.

ČAPKOVÁ, Dagmar: *Myslitelsko-vychovatelský odkaz Jana Amose Komenského (The Philosophical and Educational Heritage of Jan Amos Komenský).* Prague 1987.

ČAPKOVÁ-VOTRUBOVÁ, Dagmar – KYRÁŠEK, Jiří – ŠÁMAL, Jindřich: *Jan Amos Komenský. Život a dílo v dokumentech a v českém výtvarném umění (Jan Amos Komenský. His Life and Work in Documents and in Czech Art).* Prague 1963.

ČERVENKA, Jaromír: *Die Naturphilosophie des Johann Amos Comenius.* Prague-Hannu 1970.

ČUMA, Andrei A.: *Ian Amos Komenski i russkaya shkola (do 70 godov 18 veka).* Bratislava 1970.

DZHIBLADZE, G. N.: *Filosofiya Komenskogo.* Moscow 1982.

FISCHER, Heinz-Dietrich (Hrsg.): *„Comenius" in Konservations-lexika. Text aus „Brockhaus", „Meyer" und „Herder".* Sankt Augustin 1983.

FLOSS, Pavel: *J. A. Komenský a vědy o přírodě a člověku (Comenius and Sciences Dealing With Nature and Man).* Olomouc 1983.

FLOSS, Pavel, Jan Amos Komenský, *Od divadla věcí k dramatu člověka (Comenius. From the Theatre of Things to Human Drama).* Ostrava 1970.

GRUE-SØRENSEN, K.: *Jan Amos Comenius.* Copenhagen 1961.

HEYBERGER, Anna: *Jean Amos Comenius.* Paris 1928.

HOFMANN, Franz: *Jan Amos Komenský.* Berlin 1963.

HOFMANN, Franz: *Jan Amos Comenius, Lehrer der Nationen.* Leipzig 1975.

HORNSTEIN, Herbert: *Weisheit und Bildung. Studien zur Bildungslehre des Comenius.* Düsseldorf 1968.

HUSKOVÁ, Markéta: *Současná komeniologická pracoviště v ČSSR, památníky a pamětní síně J. A. Komenského (Current Comeniological Centres in Czechoslovakia and Monuments to Comenius).* Uherský Brod 1987.

KARŠAI, František: *Jan Amos Komenský a Slovensko (Comenius and Slovakia).* Bratislava 1970.

J. A. Komenský – Comenius. Bucharest 1958.

Jan Amos Komenský ve vývoji evropského myšlení 17. století (Comenius in the Development of 17th Century European Thought). Prague 1983.

KOPECKÝ, Jaromír – KYRÁŠEK, Jiří – PATOČKA, Jan: *Jan Amos Komenský. Nástin života a díla (Comenius. An Outline of His Life and Work).* Prague 1957.

KRASNOVSKI, A. A.: *Jan Amos Komenski.* Moscow 1953.

KROTKY, Etienne: *La pensée éducative de Coménius,* Vols. I-III. Paris 1982 – 1983.

KUMPERA, Jan – HEJNIC, Josef: *Poslední pokus českého exilu kolem Komenského o zvrat v zemích České koruny (The Last Attempt of Czech Exiles Associated With Comenius for a Turn of the Situation in the Lands of the Czech Crown).* Brno 1988.

KURDYBACHA, Łukasz: *Działalność J. A. Komeńskiego w Polsce.* Warsaw 1957.

KVAČALA, Ján: *Johann Amos Comenius*. Berlin-Leipzig-Vienna 1982.
KVAČALA, Ján: *Die pädagogische Reform des Comenius in Deutschland bis zum Ausgange des XVII. Jahrhunderts*, Vols. I-II. Berlin 1903 – 1904.
LENTZEN-DEIS, Heinrich Bodo: *Die Rolle und Bedeutung der Religion in der Pädagogik des Jan Amos Comenius*. Ratingen 1969.
LIMITI, Giuliana: *Rassegna e prospettive degli studi comeniani oggi*. Rome 1968.
LINDE, Jan M. van der: *De wereld heeft toekomst. Jan Amos Comenius over de hervorming van School, Kerk en Staat*. Kampen 1979.
LOCHMAN, Jan Milic: *Comenius*. Freiburg-Hamburg 1982.
LORDKIPANIDZE, D. O.: *Jan Amos Komenski*. 1592 – 1670. Moscow 1970.
MICHEL, Gerhard: *Schulbuch und Curricullum. Comenius im 18. Jahrhundert*. Ratingen-Kastellaun 1973.
MONROE, Will S.: *Comenius and the Beginnings of Educational Reform*. New York 1971.
MOUTOVÁ, Nicolette – POLIŠENSKÝ, Josef: *Komenský v Amsterodamu (Comenius in Amsterdam)*. Prague 1970.
NOVÁK, Jan. V. – HENDRICH, Josef: *Jan Amos Komenský. Jeho život a spisy* (Jan Amos Comenius. His Life and Writings). Prague 1932.
NOVÁKOVÁ, Julie: *Čtvrt století nad Komenským (Quarter of a Century Over Comenius)*. Uherský Brod 1989.
Otázky současné komeniologie (Questions of Contemporary Comeniology). Prague 1981.
Pädagogik und Politik. Comenius-Colloquium Bochum 1970. Ratingen-Kastellaun-Düsseldorf 1972.
PATOČKA, Jan: *Jan Amos Komenský*. Vols. I-II, Bochum 1981 – Sankt Augustin 1984.
PATOČKA, Jan: *Die Philosophie der Erziehung des J. A. Comenius*. Paderborn 1971.
PETRULLO, Salvatore: *Limiti e pregi della pedagogica di Comenio*. Catania 1974.
PLESKOT, Jaroslav: *Jan Amos Komenský's Years in Fulnek*. Prague 1972.
POPELOVÁ, Jiřina: *Filozofia Jana Amosa Komenského (The Philosophy of Jan Amos Comenius)*. Bratislava 1986.
POPELOVÁ, Jiřina: *Jana Amose Komenského cesta k Všenápravě (Jan Amos Comenius' Road to Universal Reform)*. Prague 1958.
POLIŠENSKÝ, Josef: *Jan Amos Komenský*. Prague 1973.
PRÉVOT, Jacques: *L'utopie éducative: Coménius*. Paris 1981.
ROEMECK, Renate: *Der andere Comenius*. Darmstadt 1969.
ROOD, Wilhelmus: *Comenius and the Low Countries. 1656 – 1670*. Amsterdam-Prague 1970.
RÖSSEL, Hubert: *Wörterbuch zu den tschechischen Schriften des J. A. Comenius*.

Münster 1983.

ŘÍČAN, Rudolf: *Jan Amos Komenský, muž víry, lásky a naděje (Jan Amos Comenius, a Man of Faith, Love and Hope)*. Prague 1971.

SADLER, John Edward. *J. A. Comenius and the Concept of Universal Education*. London 1966.

SCIGO, Carmelo: *Giovanni Amos Comenio, pedagogista e pansofo*. Syracuse 1959.

SCHALLER, Klaus: *Comenius*. Darmstadt 1973.

SCHALLER, Klaus (Hrsg.): *Jan Amos Komenský. Wirkung eines Werkes nach drei Jahrhunderten*. Heidelberg 1970.

SCHALLER, Klaus: *Die Pädagogik des J. A. Comenius und die Anfänge des pädagogischen Realismus im 17. Jahrhundert*. Heidelberg 1962.

SCHALLER, Klaus: *Die Pädagogik der „Mahnrufe des Elias". Das Lebenswerk des J. A. Comenius zwischen Politik und Pädagogik*. Kastellaun-Hunsrück 1978.

SCHURR, Johannes: *Comenius. Eine Einführung in die Consultatio Catholica*. Passau 1981.

SUCHODOLSKI, Bogdan: *Komeński*. Warsaw 1979.

Symposium Comenianum 1982. The Impact of J. A. Comenius on Educational Thinking and Practice. Uherský Brod 1984.

TURNBULL, G. H.: *Hartlib, Dury and Comenius*. London 1947.

Universita Karlova J. A. Komenskému 1670 – 1970 (Charles University to J. A. Comenius 1670 – 1970). Prague 1971.

URBÁNKOVÁ, Emma: *Soupis děl J. A. Komenského v československých knihovnách, archivech a muzeích (List of the Works of J. A. Comenius in Czechoslovak Libraries, Archives and Museums)*. Prague 1959.

YOUNG, Robert Fitzgibbon: *Comenius in England*. Oxford-London 1932.

Explanatory notes

Anabaptists – a radical outgrowth of the Reformation in the 16th and 17th centuries.

Antitrinitarians – in the narrow sense Christian opponents, mainly during the Reformation era, of the dogma about the Holy Trinity; in the broader sense, similar movements in the history of Christianity in general.

confessional absolutism – forced imposition of a single permitted religion in the state (mandatory unity of the religious faith professed by the ruler and by his subjects), common in the era of absolutism especially in the 17th and 18th centuries.

consistory – consultative body of a church, usually endowed with some administrative and judicial authority.

defensor – defender, protector; the Utraquist defensor was an elected protector of the church and of the interests of the non-Catholic Czech estates.

Evangelical Church of Czech Brethren – a church established in 1918 by merger of the Czech Evangelical churches of the Augsburg and Helvetian Confessions. It was also inspired by the theological doctrines of the Hussites and the Community of Brethren from the 15th to 17th centuries.

irenism – preaching of peace, endeavours to establish peace; in a narrower sense, efforts to bring about peace and conciliation between members of different churches.

Long Parliament – session of the English parliament convened in November 1640 to approve new taxes; it became the centre of opposition against Charles I and his absolute rule. It launched the English revolution and lasted until 1653. It was preceded by the Short Parliament which was called in April 1640 and was dismissed the following month.

Mannerism – originaly an Italian style of painting, sculpture and architecture between High Renaissance and the Baroque (appr. 1520 – 1610). Contemporary historiography uses this term to characterize the culture and life style at the turn of the 16th and 17th centuries, which responded to the disintegration of the Renaissance world outlook and reflected the conflicting understanding of the world at the beginning of the New Age. One of the main centres of Mannerism in Europe was the imperial court of Rudolf II in Prague (1576/ 1583 – 1612).

Pietism – a mystical movement in Protestantism, in particular its Lutheran branch, in the 17th and 18th centuries, which emerged as a reflection of the horrors of the Thirty Years' War. It was opposed to formal orthodoxy and laid stress on inner, emotional piety, exaltation, strict morality, and activity of devout laymen. In its substance, Pietism also proceeded from some aspects of the teachings of the Community of Brethren.

revelation – prophecy, forecast of the future, frequently with a topical content and serving the political aims of the advocates of revelations.

Society of Jesus – the Jesuits; a religious order founded by Ignatius Loyola in 1534 and confirmed by the Pope in 1540. The Jesuits wanted to correct the Catholic Church and imposed with great militancy Catholicism on other believers.

Socinianism – religious movement of the 16th century, which denied the dogma of the Trinity and Christ's divinity. It was founded by the Italians L. Sozzini (+ 1562) and especially his nephew F. Sozzini (+ 1604).

Index of names

Jaroslav PÁNEK

COMENIUS
Teacher of Nations

Translated from the Czech by Ivo Dvořák
Cover Daniela Slezáková
Graphic design by Tatiana Tarhaničová and Mária Budaiová

Photographs by František Chrástek, Petr Racek and Bohumil Zmítko

Editorial deadline May 1989
Published by Východoslovenské vydavateľstvo, Košice, Orbis, Prague 1991

ISBN   80-234-0045-2
(anglické vydanie)

Portrait of J. A. Comenius from the period of Enlightenment (J. Kleinhardt and J. Balzer, 1772)

Karel from Žerotín, a Moravian Estate politician and representative of the Union of the Brethren and the guardian of young J. A. Comenius

◁ Detail of the statue of J. A. Comenius by V. Makovský

Friedrich of the Palatinate, the Czech King in the years 1619 – 1620, later the Symbol of the anti-Hapsburg struggle of the Czech emigration. (A contemporary portrait)

The French statesman, Cardinal Richelieu, (A contemporary portrait)

Ferdinand II of Hapsburg, the Roman Emperor and the Czech and Hungarian King. (A contemporary portrait)

Gustav II Adolf, the King of Sweden and the leading figure of the anti-Hapsburg forces in Europe. (A contemporary portrait)

The French philosopher, René Descartes (A contemporary portrait)

Louis de Geer, a Dutch merchant in Swedish services and a sponsor of Comenius. (A contemporary portrait)

Laurens de Geer, son and successor of Louis de Geer, and the sponsor of Comenius during his stay in the Netherlands. (A contemporary portrait)

Bogusław Leszczyński, a Polish nobleman, the owner of the town of Leszno and the sponsor of the Community of the Brethren. (A contemporary portrait)

György II Rákóczi, a Transylvanian Prince. (A contemporary portrait)

František Palacký, the Czech historian and Comenius' biographer. (A contemporary portrait)

Axel Oxenstierna, a Swedish chancellor and a leading anti-Hapsburg personality during the Thirty-year War. (A contemporary portrait)

Gottfried Wilhelm Leibniz, the admirer of J. A. Comenius (A contemporary painting)

Martin Luther and John Hus Serving ▷ the Lord's Supper. (A xylograph dating from 1520)

Sermon to the Community ot the Brethren Congregation. (The Ivančice Hymn Book, 1564)

◁ Education in a Brethren family. (An illustration in the book by M. Konečný: „The Home
Preacher", 1618)

My wssickni wogeóno čelo poct=
tění sme. Kor·1·12·

Baptism in the Community of the Brethren. (The Ivančice Hymn Book, 1564)

Letters to Heaven, a socially critical work by J. A. Comenius, 1619

Ianua linguarum-The Gate of Languages, the well-known language text-book. (The title page of the edition of Elsevier Publishers in Leiden, 1640)

The Labyrinth of the World, the greatest work by J. A. Comenius in Czech language, 1631

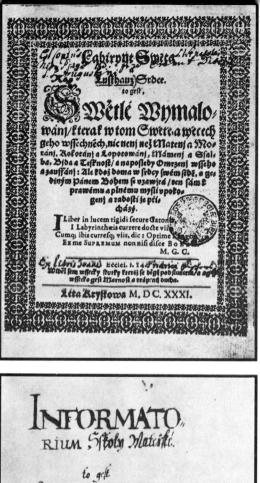

Comenius School of Infancy, the first systematic essay on pre--school education. (A Czech manuscript from the years 1630 – 1632)

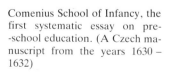

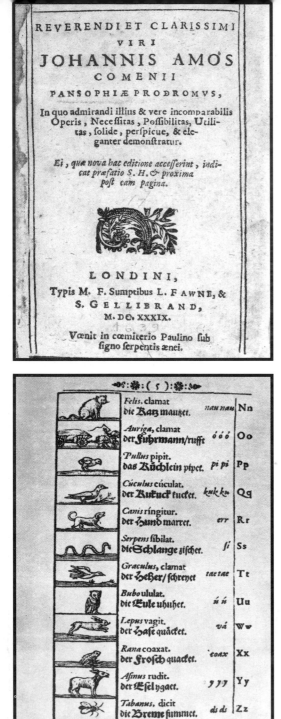

REVERENDI ET CLARISSIMI
VIRI
JOHANNIS AMOS
COMENII
PANSOPHIÆ PRODROMVS,

In quo admirandi illius & vere incomparabilis
Operis, Neceſſitas, Poſſibilitas, Utili-
tas, ſolide, perſpicue, & ele-
ganter demonſtratur.

Ei, quæ nova hac editione acceſſerint, indi-
cat præfatio S. H. & proxima
poſt eam pagina.

LONDINI,
Typis M. F. Sumptibus L. FAWNE, &
S. GELLIBRAND,
M. DC. XXXIX.

Vænit in cœmiterio Paulino ſub
ſigno ſerpentis ænei.

Pansophiae prodromus (London edition, 1639)
Via Lucis-The Way of Light, a reformation work by J. A. Comenius, compiled during his stay in London (1641 – 1642) and published in Amsterdam (1668)

The Live Alphabet from Comenius' work Orbis pictus, 1658

Via lucis – The Way of Light, the work by Comenius, written during his London stay in 1641 – 1642 and published in Amsterdam in 1668

Orbis pictus – The World in Pictures (The Norimberg edition, 1658)

SCHOLA LUDUS

Seu

ENCYCLOPÆDIA VIVA.

Hoc eft

JANUÆ LINGVARUM

praxis Scenica.

Res omnes Nomenclaturâ vestitas, & vestiendas, Sensibus ad vivum repræsentandi artificium exhibens amænum.

Ex Senecæ consilio

Non discere ista debemus, sed didicisse, per quæ majoribus paratur via.

Ergò

Vitæ præludia citò, & jucundè, seriò tamen, peragenda.

Generosis & Sapientibus, Reverendisque & Clarissimis Viris,

D. ANDREÆ de KLOBUSITZ, Sereniss. Transylv. P. P. à consiliis intimis.

D. PAULO SEMERE, Comitatûs Cassoviensis Vice-Comiti.

D. GEORGIO BARNE, Consiliario.

D. PAULO TARZALLI, Zempliniensis Diæceseos Superattendenti.

D. PAULO MEGYESI, Celsissimæ Principis Ecclesiastæ Aulico.

D. FRANCISCO VERECI, Ecclesiæ Patakinæ Pastori primario.

Illustris Patakinæ Scholæ Curatoribus dignissimis, subscripsit, S.

R 1   Hono-

Schola ludus, a work created in Sárospatak in 1653 – 1654 and published there in 1656

ANGELUS PACIS

Ad

LEGATOS PACIS

Anglos & Belgas

Bredam Missus.

Indeqve ad Omnes Christianos

per Europam,

Et mox ad omnes Populos

per Orbem totum mittendus.

Ut se sistant, belligerare desistant, Pacisqve Principi, Christo, Pacem Gentibus jam loqvuturo, locum faciant.

Anno M. DC. LXVII. Mense Majo.

Angelus pacis – The Messenger of Peace, a work admonishing reconciliation of the naval power of England and the Netherlands, 1667

A printing house (An illustration from Comenius' work Orbis pictus, 1658)

De rerum humanarum emendatione consultatio catholica – General Discourse on Reform of Human Affairs, a fundamental work of Comenius, created in the years 1645 – 70, and published by sections, beginning in 1662 and completed for the first time in 1966

London (the avenue of V. Hollar)

A portrait of Comenius ▷ on the title page of his work Opera didactica omnia, published in Amsterdam in 1657

Orbis pictus – The World in Pictures (Edition 1658)

J.A. Comenii
DIDACTICA OPERA
OMNIA.
Ab Anno 1627 ad 1657.
continuata.

Ano quo cingit Crudelis Turca Viennam enecat & Brodam Tekeliana Cohors,
ua Porta Arcensi Penetrans Cuncta obvia sternit Succendit; Domos sangvine Claustra Rigat
Sanctum Calcat eqvis Calices; Ciboria tollit atq, sepulchra aperit Vestibus Induitur
sacris Conventus, Constringit Relligiosos, Unicus eme perit, Vita, Datur, Reliquis.

Uherský Brod, a town in south-east Moravia. (A view of the burning town, dating from 1704)

Přerov, a town in central Moravia. (A drawing, dating from the first half of the 18th century)

J. A. Comenius' homeland. (South-east Moravia, around Uherský Brod on Comenius' map of Moravia, 1627)

Herbon, a university town of Hessen. (A vista from the publication by M. Zeiller: „Topographia Palatinatus Rheni," 1645)

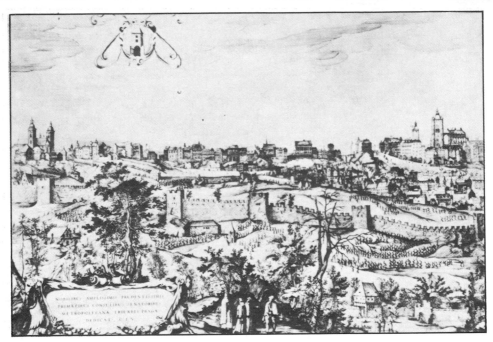

Prague (F. van Bosche, 1606)

Fulnek, a town in north Moravia. (A contemporary illustration)

The battle on the White Mountain near Prague on November 18th, 1620 (A contemporary illustration)

The Old Town Square, execution of the leaders of the Czech Estate anti Hapsburg uprising, Prague June 21st, 1621 (A contemporary illustration)

Friedrich of the Palatinate and his wife Elisabeth Stuart. (A leaflet, dating from 1619)

Leszno, a Polish town near the border of the Czech State, the home of J. A. Comenius in the years 1628 – 40, 1648 – 50 and 1654 – 56. (A contemporary illustration)

Stockholm, the capital city of the Kingdom of Sweden. (A vista from the time of Comenius)

Elblag, a town in north-east Poland, where J. A. Comenius stayed in the years 1642 – 48. (A contemporary vista)

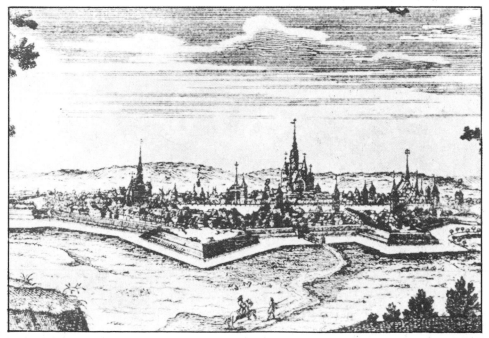

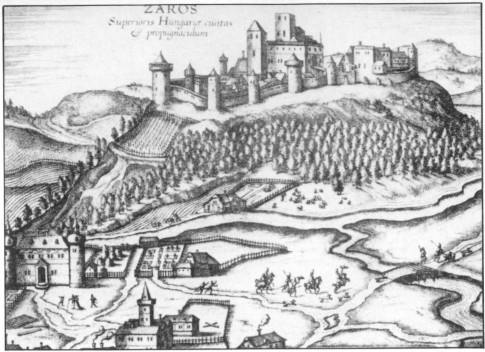

Sárospatak, a residence of Transylvanian Princes (a town in north-east Hungary) where Comenius stayed in the years 1650 – 54
Amsterdam, a Netherland town, the last home of Comenius in the years 1656 – 70. (A contemporary prospectus)

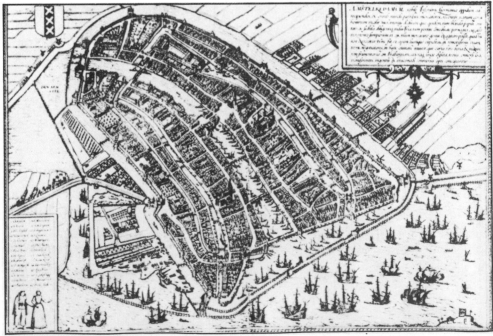

The interior decoration of a little church in Naarden

◁◁

A little church of the Walloon Reformatory Church in Naarden, a monument of J. A. Comenius

The grave of J. A. Comenius in Naarden

The Museum of J. A. Comenius in Uherský Brod – the entrance gate and statue by V. Makovský

The exhibition hall of the Museum of J. A. Comenius in Uherský Brod

The monument of J. A. Comenius in Naarden, museum exposition ▷

An emblem and a motto by Comenius (from his work Opera didactica omnia, 1657): „Let everything flow spontaneously, and violence stay in distance"

F. Bílek: J. A. Comenius bids farewell to his homeland. (A model for a statue in Prague, 1926) ▷